HOW WE LEARN TO MOVE

A REVOLUTION IN THE WAY WE COACH & PRACTICE SPORTS SKILLS

ROB GRAY, PH.D.

PERCEPTION ACTION CONSULTING & EDUCATION LLC

To Sara, for the love, support and "strong attraction".
To Angus, Molly, and Jonah for filling my life with "essential noise".
To the listeners and supporters of the Perception & Action Podcast for the
encouragement, feedback, and "emergent" discussions.

CONTENTS

PREFACE: HOW WE LEARN TO MOVE

It was about five years ago, walking around my local park on a beautiful Saturday morning, when I suddenly realized something was dreadfully wrong. On the soccer fields, kids from a local club were waiting in lines to dribble a ball around a set of *cones*. On another field, players from a nearby high school football team were waiting in a line to run through a set of *tires*. On the baseball diamond, batters were hitting balls off *tees*. On the tennis court, the instructor was tossing the ball underhand to a player attempting to repeat the same forehand stroke over and over *into an empty court*. Soccer, football, baseball and tennis are incredibly exciting, dynamic activities defined by their interpersonal actions: attacker vs defender, pitcher vs hitter, server vs receiver. It seems like almost every week we see a highlight of an athlete from one of these sports doing something new and unexpected. So, why then do we practice them in such a static, isolated, and choreographed manner? If an alien from another planet came and watched, would they think the goal of sports here on earth was to defeat inanimate pieces of rubber?

Why do we insist on teaching movement skills this way? From golf lessons to soccer practice, to learning to do pottery, the dominant view has been that we become skillful by trying to repeat the one, "correct" technique given to us by a coach or an instructor, over and over until we get it right. In baseball, tennis and golf we learn THE way to swing. In soccer and basketball, we learn THE correct way to dribble a ball. In pottery we learn THE way to position our hands. We reduce these creative, interactive, dynamic activities down to dull, isolated fundamentals so that they can be drilled and mastered. For a long time, we have assumed that decomposition and repetition rule the day if you want to be an elite performer.

In this book, I want to introduce you to a revolution in the way we think about learning to move and act in the world. A radical change in sports skills training that has inspired Chelsea coach Thomas Tuchel to have his players hold tennis balls in their hands during soccer practice[1], has lead Philadelphia Phillies' instructor Jason Ochart to conduct baseball practice using hula hoops where batters try to swing like Happy Gilmore[2], and has introduced a new practice activity to tennis great Novak Djokovic's repertoire that involves trying to deliberately pound the ball into the court[3]. A way in which there is no one correct technique. Exploration, creativity and individuality are encouraged. Repetition is not only <u>not</u> the key to becoming skillful– it is impossible. And you, yourself (not a coach or instructor) are the one with the answers.

This exciting new view of skill completely changes the way we think about learning. When we acquire a new skill, we want to harness the natural inconsistency and variability in our bodies rather than treating it as "noise" and attempting to tame it through repetition. Being skillful and creative comes through establishing a direct connection with the environment around us, not pulling away from it by becoming automatic and reflexive in our movements. Being an expert is not defined by what you have in your head but rather how effectively you relate to the world around you. As performers we want to be adaptive problem solvers and creative decision makers, not robots just executing stored programs drilled into us in practice.

There is a new role for the coach too. Rather than just running athletes through the same old drills and giving the same old instructions, in this new way of thinking about skill, coaches need to be innovative practice designers and guides through the learning process. Instead of using boring old repetition of an isolated technique, coaches adopt approaches like the Constraints Led Approach[4] and Differential Learning[5] that encourage athletes to try different things and explore (sometimes wildly) different types of movements. As we will see when we learn about these approaches, they have endless possibilities so there is lots of room for the coach to be creative and try new things too.

The revolution is also inspiring changes in other related fields. Instead of focusing on the failed endeavor of "brain training"[6], which attempts to improve things like perception, attention and decision making out of context on a small screen, innovative sports training technologies like vision occlusion glasses and movement sonification are being developed which can be used on the field while the athlete is performing their skill. Rather than just trying to recreate the "real" world, virtual reality (VR) technologies are being developed which give value added by allowing the athlete to practice things that are impractical or even impossible to do on a real field or court. This new way of thinking also presents new hope for improving an athlete's ability to avoid and recover from injuries. There is a growing body of evidence showing that encouraging a performer to execute a movement in multiple different ways (instead of repeating the one, "correct" technique) can reduce the risk of knee and elbow injuries and even concussions. Injury rehabilitation and physiotherapy are cast in the completely new light of movement exploration and increasing body awareness, rather than trying to cautiously return to where you were before with the same old set of exercises.

Finally, and returning to what I saw in the park five years ago, this revolution is changing the way we coach young athletes. Thankfully! Our traditional, fundamentals, repetition-dominated view of learning is ruining youth sports. Isolated, reductionist practice activities like running around cones or through a set of tires are boring. They remove all individuality, exploration, decision making and creativity. When kids struggle to master the "fundamentals" in sports training or physical education class they typically drop out of sports. They never get the chance to further develop the joy of movement, express their own perceptual-motor skill and movement creativity, and grow a love of actively interacting with their environment. Instead, they learn that they are "uncoordinated" and "not sporty" and move on to something else. There must be a better way. Viva la revolution!

My goals with this book

As we will see, this revolution has been going on, out of sight to most, for quite a long time. It has been led by key figures from across the globe: from Moscow, Russia to Ithaca, New York. It also involves a lot of complicated terminology and includes concepts that are not easy to grasp right away. If you dig deeper into this area, which I hope you will be inspired to do by the end of this book, you will hear intimidating-sounding terms like "Ecological Dynamics", "Dynamical Systems Theory" and

"Adaptive Complex Systems" to name a few. My goal in writing this book is not to try to explain all these complex ideas to you. Nor is it to provide a comprehensive review of this new approach to skill learning. Instead, I like to equate this book to a movie trailer. Its purpose is to introduce you to some of the main characters and ideas. To provide some evidence for this new approach by looking at a few key research studies. And along the way hopefully build some intrigue and get you excited about going to see the full movie. So, grab your popcorn!

A dominant theme throughout the book is the importance of exploration in learning. I have now been exploring this area myself for over 25 years as a researcher, professor and high-performance consultant. I have been told by many people that I have an "encyclopedic knowledge" of the literature in this area. While I secretly think they might just be referring to the fact I am old enough to have used encyclopedias, I have read a lot. I have also had a lot of practice in attempting to break the ideas down and present them in an understandable way to a broader audience, primarily through the Perception & Action Podcast, which I have been hosting and producing for over six years now. So, in the final chapter of this book, I tried to bring my experience to bear to be your guide if you choose to explore further. I have created paths for learning more about the different concepts discussed in the book with suggestions for books, videos, articles, podcast episodes and other resources.

So, I hope you enjoy it. Cheers for now. And keep 'em coupled. (We will learn what that means shortly).

THE MYTH OF THE ONE "CORRECT", REPEATABLE TECHNIQUE

T hink about the last time you were taught a new skill that involved coordinating the movement of your body. Maybe it was a golf or tennis lesson or even in a pottery class. It is likely that this involved your coach or teacher giving you lots of specific instructions about the steps you should follow and how your body should be positioned: "keep your head down", "your knees bent", "apply equal pressure with your hands", "make sure your right foot is in front of your left", etc. They were trying to convey THE ONE correct technique to you. That is their job. The instructor has the correct answer, you are there to get it from them. They then likely had you try it yourself, repeating the same movement over and over, correcting you, when necessary, until you got it down. Practice over. Class dismissed.

This type of rote repetition of the "correct" technique has long been held to be the key to learning and becoming skillful. Legendary UCLA basketball coach John Wooden once cleverly proclaimed that: "The eight laws of learning are explanation, demonstration, imitation, repetition, repetition, repetition, and repetition"[1]. Repetition in learning a new skill is the equivalent of location in real estate. It has also been given parental status in successful learning: repetition is "the mother of skill" according to Tony Robbins[2] and the "father of action" in Zig Ziglar's[3] view. It is thought to be irreplaceable as a method for learning. In his book "The Talent Code"[4], Daniel Coyle states that "there is no substitute for attentive repetition". I could go on with quotes spanning the gamut from baseball legend Reggie Jackson[5] to painter Bob Ross[6]. Apparently, the importance of repetition bears repeating!

Despite this entrenched view of the primacy of repetition, there is an ever-growing revolution out there against it. Its followers not only believe that repetition of the correct technique is not the key to skilled performance and learning to move – they believe that repetition of movement is not even possible. But we will get to that. To understand the alternative view of how we learn to coordinate our movements we need to start in Moscow, Russia in the early 1900s with an unconventional scientist who decided that when he couldn't find the answers he was looking for, he would just change the question.

The Legend of Bernstein's Hammer

Nikolai Bernstein (1896-1966) was a self-taught, Soviet scientist on a quest to better understand how human beings controlled their movements. His career was unorthodox in many ways including the fact that he somehow received a Doctoral degree in 1926 without ever submitting a written dissertation. But perhaps the most unique aspect of the path he took was that it was equally shaped by the pressures of academic theory and practical application. In 1922, after returning from serving with the Red Army in World War I, Bernstein was hired by the Soviet Central Institute of Labor to study and help improve the productivity of their manual laborers. One of his first assignments was to study blacksmiths cutting sheet metal by hitting a chisel with a hammer[7]. Why did some blacksmiths seem to hit the exact same spot on the chisel head, cutting the metal more quickly and precisely, while others were more variable? The conventional wisdom at the time was the now familiar repetition idea: the lesser skilled workers had not yet learned to reliably repeat the one correct hammering technique.

But luckily, Bernstein was a "I want to see for myself" kind of person. In his opinion, the key to understanding movement was being able to first measure it. To tackle this problem, he adapted a new technique for measuring movement called cyclography. This involved attaching a bunch of light bulbs to key points on the performer's body then having them repeat their skill over and over while filming it using a camera with a high-speed shutter. If this sounds vaguely like the technique used today to create CGI characters like Gollum in the Lord of the Rings, it is because it uses the same basic principles. Using this cyclography method with his blacksmiths, Bernstein generated a series of images like the one shown in Figure 1.1. The moving hammer created paths of light for both the hammer and parts of the blacksmith's body that he could use to calculate the trajectories of movement, meticulously, by hand.

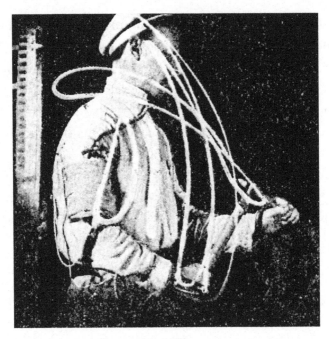

*Figure 1.1 - Nikolai Bernstein's Use of Cyclography
to Analyze the Movement of a Blacksmith.*

What did Bernstein find? First, he compared the movement traces for a novice and a highly experienced blacksmith. The novice's results seemed to confirm the conventional repetition story: they had highly variable outcomes (they did not consistently hit the head of the chisel in the same spot) because they had highly variable movements (the path the hammer followed on the way to the chisel was different on every strike). Novices were not as skillful because their movement was not repeatable. Case closed. But wait, what about the expert blacksmith? The cyclographic results for this participant (shown in Figure 1.2) have since become one of the most iconic images in the field of movement science. The lines don't fit so we must acquit. As can be seen in this figure, which shows two separate hammer strikes, the experienced blacksmith hit the same spot on the chisel but not by repeating the same movement every time. Bernstein coined this surprising result "repetition without repetition". We repeat an action outcome but not by repeating the movement that produced it.

Figure 1.2 - "Repetition without Repetition". Nikolai Bernstein's movement analysis of two hammer swings made by a skilled blacksmith. He repeats the same outcome (accurately hitting the chisel) but NOT by repeating the same movement.

Jumping ahead about 100 years, we see a very similar story when looking at another type of manual craft: pottery. Gandon and colleagues[8] used video recordings to identify the hand positions used by professional potters when asked to craft a sphere (Figure 1.3). They compared a group of seven French and eight Indian potters. When looking at the final product produced, the outcomes were essentially the same: there were no significant differences in the geometry of the spheres created by the different potters. But looking at the hand positions used to produce the spheres gave a very different story. The bottom of Figure 1.3 shows the correlations between hand positions for the 13 potters.

There are two things we can see here. First, if the potters were using the same hand techniques to produce the spherical pot, then this figure should contain a series of black squares (indicating high positive correlations). But clearly it does not – again, repetition <u>without</u> repetition! Second, it is apparent there are more black squares in the top left and bottom right quadrants of the image. These are the correlations between potters from the same country, which are stronger. So, there seems to be a cultural similarity in the hand movements used. This is an important point I will return to in Chapter 4. We don't repeat our movements, but they are not completely random and variable either. They are shaped by the constraints of our environment (including our culture). But back to Moscow first..

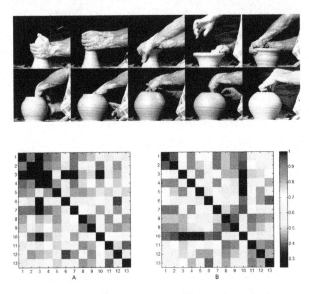

Figure 1.3 - Top panel: Making a "sphere" in pottery. Bottom panels: Correlations between the hand movements used to produce a sphere between 13 different potters (1-7 from France and 8-13 from India) with the grey scale shown on the right.

Bernstein's second key finding from his work with the blacksmiths came when he looked at the movements of their body. Traditional thinking about how we control a fast and powerful skill like swinging a hammer has always been that it must involve a ballistic, open-loop movement. Think shooting a cannonball out of a cannon. We perform the skill by planning the movement beforehand (aiming the cannon), initiating it (lighting the wick) and then letting it run, on its own, without any changes (watching the cannonball fly towards the target). Set it and forget it. If we have mastered the one correct, highly repeatable technique why would we need to alter anything? But Bernstein found something different. Specifically, when he compared the shoulder and elbow joint movements to that of the hammer, the experienced blacksmith's body movements were more variable than the movements of the hammer. That is like making a cannonball turn in mid-air when you see its going off target. Instead of using a ballistic movement that wasn't altered after it began, he concluded that the joints were working together on the fly, to correct each other's errors and keep the hammer on target. Bernstein's expert blacksmith wasn't armed with a cannon – he had guided missiles!

So, Bernstein had thrown a wrench (or rather a hammer) into the works of motor control theory and started the anti-repetition revolution. Skilled performance did not involve one correct movement technique. Instead, it involved using a slightly different technique with every execution. The key to becoming skillful was not strict repetition. Instead, it was repetition without repetition – learning to produce the same outcome by using different movements. What happened after a movement started was as important, if not more, than the planning that was done beforehand. We will hear a lot more from Bernstein later but let's first move from the workshop to the sports field. Surely, elite athletes must be using the same "correct" technique when winning world championships or gold medals?

Coordination Profiling & What Gets Lost in the Average

Since Bernstein's studies of blacksmiths in the 1920's, technology for capturing and measuring human movements has come a long way. Along with increases in recording rates and measurement precision, one of the biggest changes has been the automatization of the analysis process. Whereas Bernstein spent hours aligning the images on graph paper and calculating the body positions by hand (doing so 500 hundred times for every second of recorded movement), modern systems are equipped with analysis software that can spit out the same calculations within seconds. This has allowed movement researchers to do something we always push for in science: have larger sample sizes in our studies. Instead of having just two blacksmiths, we could easily study the movements of 20 or 100. But while this is obvious progress, it has also served to perpetuate the myth of the one correct technique.

Most of the modern history of movement science has been the study of groups. For example, consider the 2008 study by Zheng and colleagues[9] examining swing technique in golf. For this, 18 PGA Tour Professionals and 18 amateurs participated. They were each equipped with markers from a motion tracking system and their different body positions during the swing were compared. On the surface, this seems like an obvious way to understand what makes an elite golfer. By comparing groups of different skill levels, we can pull out features of the technique that differ between them, with the assumption that what the professionals are doing is the "correct" technique. And using groups, instead of individuals, removes the possibility that we just picked an unorthodox expert (maybe Bernstein's blacksmith was an oddball?) and allows us to use standard statistical methods to test whether the differences are significant. K. Anders Ericsson, the late professor of psychology at Florida State University and of deliberate practice fame, dubbed this type of group comparison the "expert-performance approach" and felt it was the critical first step in understanding the nature of expertise[10].

And if we look at the result of the aforementioned golf study it seems to provide exactly what we were looking for. At the peak of the backswing, the professional golfers had significantly larger bend in their elbow, larger shoulder movement away from the side of the body, and greater rotation of their trunk as compared to the amateurs. For those readers looking for the exact recipe for an elite golf swing, the average values for these body movements were 130, 66, and 60 degrees, respectively. Voila! We have identified the characteristics of the "correct" expert technique for a golf swing. Elite golfers all share these key movement features and so golf instruction should focus on increasing elbow bend, shoulder movement and trunk rotation.

But wait a second. Let's consider what these values are telling us. These measurements of body movements are the averages for a group of 18 players. Because of the way averages work we would get the same average value if all 18 golfers used the identical, correct technique, if 9 used large (above average) body movements and 9 used small movements, or if the golfers ranged from small to large in their movements. So, which is it? Look at the photographs of the different golfers at peak backswing in

Figure 1.4 and you be the judge. Clearly, even with the naked eye we can see that these golfers are not doing the same movements. A bit straighter arm here, a bit more bent wrist there, never mind where the clubhead is pointing. The fact that we can put one number (an average) on an expert's movements does not mean that there is one correct technique, and all experts do the same thing.

*Figure 1.4 - Comparison of different club positions
at the top of the backswing in golf*

So, if we don't group elite athletes together what can we do instead? Rather than trying to focus on what they do the same, how can we explore what they do differently? An interesting alternative to looking at average movements is a technique developed by Wolfgang Schollhorn and colleagues called coordination profiling[11]. In this approach, a small number of participants are asked to perform multiple executions of their skill, with movement data recorded. Machine learning algorithms are then trained to learn and identify the movement patterns of each performer. So, like in creating a psychological profile for a serial killer, we are creating a coordination profile for an elite athlete.

. . .

What do we find when we use this approach? First, think about what we would get if there really was one correct, repeatable technique. Coordination profiling would be impossible because every elite athlete would produce essentially the same data. But you can probably guess by now, that's not at all what we see. In a 1998 study, Schollhorn and Bauer developed coordination profiles for eight male and 19 female javelin throwers competing at either the national or international level. Remarkably the throwing style of the different athletes could be reliably identified even over a three-year period of training. They could be picked out of the suspect lineup every time! What's more, the number of different profiles (that is, the amount of variability between the performers) was larger for the more skilled international-level athletes as compared to the national ones. Similar findings can be seen in a 2012 study[12] looking at elite male swimmers. Here again, the swimmers could be classified into different coordination styles that differed in terms of parameters like the glide time under water, the balance in the stroke and the symmetry of breathing. Finally, Horst and colleagues[13] recently found that coordination profiling can even work across different skills. Specifically, they were able to reliably identify individual decathletes in one throwing discipline (for example, the shot put or the discus) using an algorithm trained with data from a different discipline (the javelin). Clearly, if we can so readily distinguish one elite athlete from another based solely on their pattern of movement, they are not all moving in the same way.

The Variability Revolution

Bernstein's hammer and looking under the cover of averages with coordination profiling have revealed that variability, not repeatability or repetition, rules the day in skilled performance. The one correct technique instructors have been trying to teach us on all those fields, courts, rinks and work benches, for all these long years, is a myth. Skillful movers in the same discipline do not all coordinate their movements in the same way – there is significant *inter*-movement variability between performers. Skillful movers do not achieve their goal by moving the same way every time - there is significant *intra*- movement variability within performers. While the loss of the comfort of rote repetition may sound daunting, as we will see in the next chapter, it fits perfectly with what the body was designed to do.

2

WE ARE BUILT TO PRODUCE AND DETECT VARIATION

How regular should your heartbeat be? "Very" is the answer I think most people would give. But what if I told you that having perfect repetition of your heartbeat can be a dangerous sign that you have a serious medical problem? Think about heart activity represented on an EKG monitor. We get a peak in the wave, it goes back down, then another peak occurs, etc. If we measure the time between those peaks, we will get a value, called the R-R interval, that is between about 0.6-1.2 seconds for most people. Now let's keep measuring that value over and over for a few minutes. Is it the same every time? Does your heart beat like a metronome? No... well, at least hopefully not! Heart rate variability (HRV)[1] is a measure of the fluctuation in the time between consecutive beats of your heart. Although the exact value is highly individual, HRV is not zero. It ranges between about 30-100 milliseconds depending on a host of factors including gender and age. Elite athletes have a higher HRV than non-athletes. Our HRV decreases when we are put in stressful, high-pressure situations. The decrease in HRV under pressure distinguishes between clutch (small decrease) performers and those that "choke" under pressure (big decrease)[2]. Having a low HRV can be an indicator of cardiovascular disease and predict sudden cardiac arrest. HRV is just one example of how the human body produces variability. A lack of variability is bad. We will get to the "why?" shortly, but let's look at another example first.

When intently fixating on an object, like a basketball hoop during a free throw, your eyes are not completely still. When we "lock our eyes" on a target, slight movements of our head produce image jitter - movement of the image back and forth on the eye[3]. This movement is small – if you hold your arm straight out the image moves back and forth about 1/3 the width of your thumbnail every second–but it seems to serve some important functions. First, it prevents the object from disappearing! A well-studied phenomenon in perception research is perceptual fading[4] – the tendency for objects that are completely stabilized on the eye (using equipment like a head rest) to disappear from consciousness. Participants report it is no longer there even though it is still on the screen in front of them! This occurs because our sensory systems stop signaling our brain when there is nothing changing. Are you wearing a watch right now? How do you know? Are you getting a tactile sensation like you would if an insect landed on your arm? No. That stopped shortly after you put the watch on. If nothing is changing, there is no new information, so our senses stop telling us about it. Martin Regan and colleagues have shown that image jitter also helps us perceive objects moving towards us. Without it, the sensory output we get is highly non-linear because it does not change systematically as the input signal changes.

. . .

Finally, it was long believed that this image jitter was produced only by head movements while our eyes themselves remained still. As it turns out, that is not true either. The development of higher resolution eye tracking equipment has revealed the presence of microsaccades[5] - tiny movements of our eyes that occur when we are trying our best to keep them perfectly still. In an interesting series of studies, Michele Rucci and colleagues have shown that these small movements of our eyes are functional. For example, when they are removed, we are not as good at seeing the fine details in images. The rate of these microsaccades also increases as the task we are doing gets more difficult suggesting that they distinguish between just looking at something from really seeing it - that is picking up and using the information in the image.

Our bodies produce variable patterns and movements. This is true even when doing things we would expect to be consistent and regular like the beat of our heart or keeping our eyes still, never mind complex motor skills like hitting a ball. Our bodies are also designed to detect variation in our environment. Our senses adapt quickly to things that don't change. We have two eyes and two ears so that we detect differences between the incoming signals. A sound coming from the left hits the left ear slightly earlier than it hits the right ear -a minuscule variation that allows us to localize sounds. Because our eyes are separated by about two inches, the images that arrive vary slightly in each eye. We use this information to perceive depth and it is the basis of 3D movie technology. Viva la difference! Why are we wired this way? What is the value of all this variability?

Variability as Noise

The traditional view of movement variability is an extension of Information Theory[6] developed by Charles Shannon to understand telecommunication. Imagine that you and a friend are talking on the phone (if you still even do that!) and there is poor reception. Your friend (the information source) is trying to send you a message via a transmitter (their phone). The signal is a systematic pattern in an acoustic signal. Your job is to reliably receive and understand this signal so you can make a response. But there is something being added to make your life difficult – random, unsystematic variability in the acoustic signal, noise. These random variations are distorting the signal (making it noisy) and are something we want to get rid of by redialing, moving to a new location, or buying a new phone.

As we have already established, this type of "noisy" variability seems to be, for some crazy reason, a design feature of the human body. Along with the specific examples we already seen, our entire nervous system is inherently noisy, from the bottom to the top[7]. Substantial variability occurs in the movement of ions (positively charged atoms). Sometimes the ion channels in our brain seem to open and let them through when they should, but sometimes they don't. Movement of these ions allows the different parts of your brain to "talk to" each other by generating action potentials – a spike in electrical activity in response to some event. These occur over a background of random electrical potentials, seemingly nonfunctional and random changes in the electrical activity your body creates. When action potentials are generated, much like with HRV, their timing seems to be highly imprecise and variable. And, on and on it goes. We apparently bought ourselves a very bad, noisy phone!

. . .

Following Shannon's theory, these different sources of variability in our bodily processes have long been conceptualized as "noise". Something bad that we need to get rid of if we want the system to function at a high level. How do we get rid of it? Well, this is one of the main things repetition is thought to achieve. The high variability in movement from execution to execution we see in novice performers is noise – fluctuations that are hiding the true signal, the correct technique. They represent an error in the system that is generating the movement. Repeating the same movement over and over boosts the signal while reducing the noise (that annoying variation in movement).

Before we get to an alternative view of the role of variability, let's look at an interesting sporting example of noisy signals. Being a talented soccer player requires you to know what your feet are doing. But how much does that depend on the shoes you are wearing? In an interesting study published in 2003[8], Waddington and Adams asked a group of 22 international-level soccer players to reproduce different foot positions while blindfolded. So, for example, on one trial they might be asked to roll their ankle 30 degrees inwards while on another they might be asked to roll it 15 degrees outwards. They were asked to do this in three different conditions: while standing barefoot, while wearing soccer shoes with the typical smooth insoles, and while wearing soccer shoes with insoles that were covered in small, textured bumps.

What did they find? When the players switched from barefoot to wearing the standard shoes with smooth insoles the angle production accuracy decreased significantly, by about 5%. This is not surprising. Adding rubber cleats, socks and insoles between your feet and the ground should weaken the tactile signals you receive on contact – a critical source of sensory information particularly when you don't have vision. What happened when they switched from smooth to bumpy insoles? Surely, this should make things worse. The bumps are going to make the tactile signal you receive when moving your feet around noisy and variable – think about driving your car over a road being repaved. But that is not what was found. Adding the bumps to the insole significantly improved performance such that it was slightly better than the level achieved when standing barefoot. What is going on here? The human nervous system is riddled with sources of noise and adding even more helps. Maybe we need to look at variability in a different light.

Variability as "Essential Noise"

Why might variability – inconsistency – non-repeatability – noise be a beneficial design feature of the human body? To understand this idea let's look at some noisy images. Figure 2.1a shows a pattern (three horizontal bars, the signal) that is difficult to see. Let's make it a little clearer. Voila, Figure 2.1b. How did we improve the visibility of the image? By adding noise. The only difference between these two images is that in (b), a large number of randomly positioned dots have been added. Little dots placed in random locations should be unhelpful noise, like when you turn your TV on and the cable is out. The additional dots are just as likely to fall on top of the bars as there are to fall in the space between them. Why do they make the three bars easier to see?

18

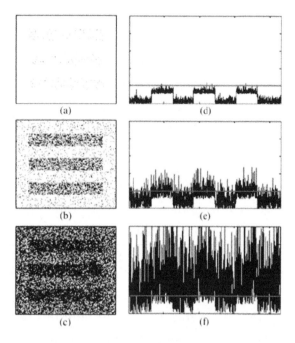

Figure 2.1 - An example of stochastic resonance. The three horizontal bars in (a) are made more visible by adding noise (randomly positioned dots) in (b). From Dylov et al (2011).

What we have here is an example of what is called "stochastic resonance". Breaking this term down, stochastic is basically a fancy word for random (that's the dots we added) while resonance is a term that comes from acoustics. I think most readers will have seen a demo of the phenomenon of auditory resonance but if you haven't, take a short break and go here[9]. If we play a sound at the right frequency (pitch) we can cause objects to start to vibrate. So, the basic idea is that if we add the right thing it can resonate with the signal inside and pull it out. And that's what is happening in the images in Figure 2.1. The noisy dots added in (b) are resonating with the weak signal to help to better construct it. But critically there is a sweet spot here. Adding too much noise (as shown in Figure 2.1c) will eventually make the signal less visible again. As we will see in Chapter 8, finding the right amount of noise seems to be one of the key skills a coach needs to have when applying an increasingly popular sports training method called Differential Learning. But we will get to that.

Let's now use stochastic resonance to explain the mystery of the bumpy insoles. When a soccer player rolls their ankle back and forth, they are going to feel pressure on the soles of their feet that provides tactile information about their foot position. As I roll my right foot inwards, I get a slightly more pressure on the left side of my sole then on the right. As I roll it more this imbalance of pressure will get larger and larger until all the pressure is on the inner, left half of my foot. Now what happens if I add a uniform surface (like a smooth insole) between my foot and the ground? It is like adding a mattress in the story of the Princess and the Pea. The insole is going to weaken or dampen the force coming from the ground, making me less able to notice the small differences, and less accurate at judging the position of my foot. Putting randomly positioned bumps on the insole is equivalent to adding the dots in Figure 2.1. Although it is effectively adding noise, as Keith Davids and colleagues[10] proposed, it is very likely that it produced stochastic resonance which enhanced the force signal coming from the ground. The improved ability to judge foot angle certainly supports this idea. Maybe one of the reasons our nervous system is riddled with noise is because it's actually essential for perceiving our environment – it helps to pull signals out, make them resonate. Let's explore the possible benefits of variability further by returning to the legend of Bernstein's hammer.

. . .

Variability, Adaptability & Degeneracy

Why did Bernstein's blacksmith swing the hammer slightly differently every time? Surely if I want to produce the same outcome, under the same conditions, the best strategy would be to repeat the same movement every time. Bernstein himself identified the flaw with this logic: the "same" in the middle. When we move the conditions are never the same. Just ask tennis great Rafael Nadal:

"You might think that after millions and millions of balls I've hit, I'd have the basic shots of tennis show up, that reliably hitting a true, smooth clean shot every time would be a piece of cake. But it isn't. Not just because every day you wake up feeling differently, but because *every shot is different; every single one*. From the moment the ball is in motion, it comes at you at an infinitesimal number of angles and speeds, with more topspin, or backspin, or flatter or higher. The differences might be minute, microscopic, but so are the variations your body makes—shoulders, elbows, wrists, hips, ankles, knees—in every shot. And there are so many other factors—the weather, the surface, the rival. No ball arrives the same as another; no shot is identical."[11] This is an example of a problem that our motor system must solve which Bernstein dubbed "context conditioned variability."[12]

Simply put, movements of our body do not occur in vacuum. As Nadal so nicely said, they live within the context of a set of changing internal and external factors such that the same commands sent to our spinal cord and muscles will not always result in the same movement outcomes. Weather conditions, different shot directions and opponent's tendencies provide an ever-changing external context while things like fatigue, growth, and micro traumas in muscles from a workout the day before create a backdrop of variability from the inside. So, we need to revise the statement we made at the start of this section. If I want to produce the same outcome, under ever- changing conditions, I have to use a different movement every time.

Now we have hit the very crux of the reason there is all this variability going on in our body, from the movement of ions to the movement of our limbs. With variability comes adaptability! Being able to produce slightly different, variable patterns allows us to adapt to changes in our environment - both internal and external. If the problems of movement are always changing (even for one of the greatest tennis players in history), then we need to have multiple solutions.

Think about it. If this were not the case. If there was only one correct way to do things, we would break one of the fundamental laws of learning: "you never forget how to ride a bike". I don't know about you but, in my life, I have sometimes gone years between hopping back on a bicycle. During those periods I may have grown taller, gained or lost a few pounds (more likely the former), become less flexible, gotten stronger as a result of the gym membership I was given as a gift, etc. If I repeated the same forces and patterns of muscle activity, I used the last time I was on a bike (the one "correct" solution) I would be down on the ground or over the handlebars in a second. The problem has transformed in the intervening years off the bike, so we need a different movement solution.

. . .

This adaptability through having multiple, variable solutions to achieve the same goal is a fundamental feature found throughout nature, termed "biological degeneracy". A "degenerate" is a highly abnormal person. Someone who has moved so far from the norms of society that they are considered being fatally flawed. That sounds even worse than "noise"! How can that be good? Well, it is being used here again to dispel the myth of the one correct, normal solution. Degeneracy occurs in a system when components that are structurally dissimilar can perform similar functions – they are effectively interchangeable. It is like building something out of Legos. The small little bricks are different from the big, long bricks, but in a pinch one can substitute for the other. By moving away from the one obvious, normal solution towards more "degenerate" solutions we can adapt to changes in our environment (e.g., lost Legos).

A prime example of biological degeneracy is in your genetic code. Within your DNA are codes for amino acids, the building blocks of protein. In genetics, these codes are three letter combinations called codons. Examples include GAA, GGU, UCA. You would think that in building the system we would make one code for each type of amino acid, kind of like a lock and key. But that is not the way it works. For example, codons GAA and GAG, two structurally different DNA sequences, can both serve as the code for glutamic acid, the most prevalent excitatory neurotransmitter in your brain. Why do things work this way? Because having more than one code (more than one solution) to achieve the same outcome makes us robust and adaptable. Degenerate solutions can compensate for each other when one fails, for example due to a virus or infection that attacks our genes.

. . .

Having multiple solutions creates the advantageous state of *redundancy*. We are not reliant on any one solution. Others are waiting in the wings to do the same job. We can adapt. We can match the variability in the context Bernstein identified with the variability in our movement solutions. If the ball Rafael Nadal is about to play goes in a direction that doesn't allow for a typical backhand, he has the "degenerate" between the legs shot ready to step in and get the ball back over the net. Same successful outcome under different conditions because of different (not the same, repeatable) solutions. Variability is a beneficial design feature that allows us to adapt and keep achieving our goals. It also seems to help prevent us from getting hurt.

Variability as a Pain Reduction & Injury Prevention Mechanism

Why do we get injured when playing sports? The traditional view is that injuries occur for two reasons: you are doing it wrong and/or you are doing it too much. "Don't let your knees go past your toes". "Your shoulder is flying open", aka you are not using the correct technique. "The pitcher threw too many pitches in the game". "You were trying to lift too much weight". In other words, you are overloading the system. Are there any alternatives to preventing injury than just chasing the unicorn of repeatability and telling athletes to do less?

In 2004, James proposed an interesting twist on these traditional explanations for sports injuries[13] . The "variability-overuse hypothesis" starts with the same basic concept: Repeated application of load eventually leads to tissue breakdown and injury. Don't do it too much. But then it adds a new twist that fits nicely with the theme of this chapter: this breakdown will occur when there is not enough variability in movement to allow for adaptation. So, the problem is not that you are not doing it the one, correct way. In fact, trying to do that, trying to have a highly consistent, repeatable movement is likely to increase the chance of injury, not decrease it.

Why might this be the case? Think about jumping off a box and landing on the ground. If we performed this movement the same way every time, we would stress the same muscles, tissues, bones, etc. in the same way every time. Ouch! Allowing for slight variations in the technique used, in terms of direction, location, magnitude and frequency of the muscle activity involved, creates a broader distribution of stressors which reduces the chance of injury. Having variability also allows the different parts to work together and compensate for each other's errors.

We can see an interesting application of these ideas in a study designed to reduce pain in runners by Bonacci and colleagues[14]. Patellofemoral pain (PFP) or what is more commonly known as "runner's knee," is chronic pain around or behind the kneecap that gets worsened by load bearing activities like running. Consistent with the variability overuse hypothesis, it has been shown that when you measure the angles of the ankle, knee and hips joints in runners with PFP, they have less variability in the movement of joints as compared to healthy runners. So, like adding the random dots in Figure 3 or putting bumps on soccer shoe insoles, could we help these runners by making them more variable?! That is exactly what these authors found. Training the PFP runners to increase their cadence by running to the beat of a metronome on a treadmill lead to an increase in the joint variability while running and a significant reduction in ratings of knee pain. We will see more examples of this novel approach to injury prevention in Chapter 14.

So, variability in our systems is not unwanted noise. It is an essential and protective design feature that makes us robust and adaptable. It gives us multiple, redundant solutions to solve the problems created by our complex, ever-changing environment. But how do we learn to harness this variability? How do we learn to come up with movement solutions to achieve our goals?

3

THE BUSINESS OF PRODUCING MOVEMENTS & WHY WE DON'T NEED A BOSS

"It is clear that the basic difficulties for coordination consist precisely in the extreme abundance of degrees of freedom, with which the nervous centre is not at first in a position to deal."

- Nikolai Bernstein[7]

I f the variability in our body allows us to move in multiple different ways to achieve the same goal, how then do we choose which way to move? This essential question, coined the *degrees of freedom of problem* by Bernstein, remains one of the most important questions in movement science. This wonderful degeneracy and redundancy we discussed in Chapter 2 creates a fundamental problem we know human beings struggle with: too much choice! Think about making a forehand stroke in tennis. As illustrated in Figure 3.1, you can do this in almost an infinite number of different ways. You could just rotate your arm around your shoulder joint. Or you could use some shoulder rotation plus some lower arm rotation around your elbow joint. Or you could combine rotation around the shoulder, rotation around the elbow joint, and rotation of your hand around the wrist joint, with a host of different choices for the amounts of each. These different rotational movements that can be used are what Bernstein called "degrees of freedom" – you are free to choose the values that they have.

Figure 3.1 - Bernstein's Degrees of Freedom
problem illustrated for a tennis stroke.

But how do we choose? When we are first learning a new skill, it is like we are standing in front of a microwave. I could heat my food on medium for 10 minutes or on high for 5. Or should I be using the defrost setting? Ah, forget it, I am just going to press the "popcorn" button! To understand how we solve this fundamental problem of coordination, making our different body parts move together to achieve our goal, let's get into the business of motor control.

Over the years, there have been many analogies used to describe how we move and learn to control our movements. In Bernstein's time it was a "cortical keyboard": the control of movement was conceptualized as a piano being played by a musician inside our brain (often called the homunculus or little man). When the pianist pressed a key on the keyboard, it would send a particular set of commands down to the spinal cord and muscles, which would cause a particular movement to occur. Becoming skillful was all about picking the right piece of music to play at the right time and learning to flawlessly repeat it.

Currently, for most people, the control of action involves the world's greatest super-computer. Learning to control movement relies on building extensive memory stores of knowledge (hard drive), developing the processing power to interpret sensory information (CPU) and being able to hold information in working memory to execute motor programs (RAM). But the analogy I want to focus on here is the idea that movement control is like running a business. Welcome to "Let's Move Incorporated"!

Like any good business, the successful control of action has long been thought to come from the top, via the boss, the CEO, the head honcho —The Central Executive. The workers in the business are organized and productive because they follow the executive orders from above. Your body's business organizational chart is shown in Figure 3.2. The company functions via a structure of hierarchical, top-down control. Getting our product (movement) out of the door relies on the higher centers controlling the lower centers. The Central Executive (the cerebral cortex) gives the overall plan of action after receiving information from the sensory areas of the brain. The manager (the Motor Cortex) works on the specifics needed to carry out the plan (e.g., which muscles need to be used). Finally, the assembly line workers (in the brainstem and spinal cord) actually do the work and execute the movements. Learning to move successfully primarily comes from having an effective boss: one that can take in and process all the information and anticipate what needs to be done next.

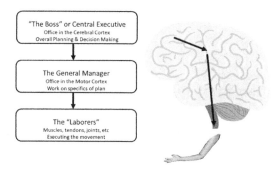

*Figure 3.2 -The Hierarchical Business Model of
Producing Movements*

From the hierarchical structure in our business, we can also create a flow chart of the processes involved in action production like the one shown in Figure 3.3. The Perception department takes in the current market reports. The Cognition department meets in the boardroom to analyze and interpret them. The Decision Making department uses this analysis to come up with a plan of action for the next quarter. And, finally, this business plan is executed by the Motor Control department. A key feature of this organization is its linearity: processes flow in a distinct order, one to the other, with each department working relatively independently from the others. The Motor Control department frequently gets annoyed when the Decision Making department makes plans without asking them first!

Figure 3.3 - The Linear flow of Processes in the
Traditional Business Model

Solving Bernstein's degrees-of-freedom problem is achieved by the Central Executive, and the associated Cognition and Decision Making departments, developing a plan for what all the muscles and joints should be doing during the movement. Richard Schmidt proposed the most well-developed version of this approach in what he called the Generalized Motor Program or GMP[1]. A GMP is a representation for a particular motor action, stored in your memory, which specifies the values for each of the degrees of freedom you need when moving. In a forehand shot in tennis, it might be something like: rotate around shoulder 30 degrees, then around elbow 20 degrees then around wrist by 15 degrees. It is a specific set of detailed commands given by the central controller to the workers below (the joints and muscles).

How do we come up with this business plan or GMP? From our business model, we can derive some key training principles we can use for our next professional development day. The first is modularity or separability. Because our organizational structure is highly linear and hierarchical, we can train and develop the different departments (or modules) separately from each other. One department can complete a course on business analytics while another does a team building exercise. We have smartly designed a business that can be broken into parts, trained and then put back together.

The second key training principle is context independence. The success of our business relies heavily on the general abilities of the people working in the different departments. Analogous to the leadership, communication, data analysis, and teamwork we see in a real business, here we have general skills like perception, attention, working memory and decision making. These are all abilities and skills that can apply to any business regardless of the product being made so they do not need to be trained specifically, in context. The specifics of the type of movement we are making (e.g., whether we are moving by running, skating or skiing) is thought to be not critical for improving these general abilities.

Sports skills training has a long history of using practice drills that are built on this traditional business model of action control. First, consider some examples of modularity. Hitting a ball off a tee in baseball and dribbling through cones in soccer involve training the Motor Control department separately from perception and decision making. In both cases, the information I need to perceive during the game (the flight of the ball or the movement of a defender) has been removed and there are no decisions involved (I am swinging every time and I am told by my coach beforehand to "go right" around the cones). We often call this learning the technique or "the fundamentals". Similarly, we can try to train the Perception and Decision Making departments separately from motor control. A common example of this in sports is the use of video to help an athlete learn what to "look for". A football quarterback watches unfolding plays and is asked to give a verbal response about what they would do: "I would throw deep" or "I would dump the ball off to the running back".

In terms of context independence, it has long been believed that it is possible to improve an athlete's performance by training their general, multi-purpose perceptual-motor abilities. A prime example is "vision training" designed to improve your ability to see details in an image, perceive the depth of objects by adjusting your focus and track moving objects by moving your eyes. The concept was first introduced over 40 years ago with training programs like "Eyerobics" and "Sports Vision" and is still quite popular today. Critically, the stimuli used in this type of training (beads on strings, moving circles on a computer screen, charts with letters on them, etc.) are not sports specific. They do not contain the information an athlete uses to control their actual movements in the game. They lack context because in our business model specificity is unnecessary for improving these general abilities.

Another contextually independent type of training that has been used in sports for many years are eye-hand coordination drills. If you want to go the cheap route you can bounce tennis balls off a wall and try to catch them with one hand. If you have some money to spend you can invest in Dynavision, which first came on the market in the late 1990s. This product is a 5-foot x 4-foot board on which are mounted 64 red buttons that can be illuminated and turned off by touch. A light is turned on at a random location on the board and the user must locate and strike it with the hand as quickly as possible. Again, this follows our business model of training general abilities ("eye-hand coordination", "reaction time", "peripheral vision") using completely abstract, out of context stimuli. You don't play against little lights in many sports, last time I checked! Following in the footsteps of products like Dynavision, as shown in Figure 3.4, there is currently a rapidly growing industry of perceptual-cognitive training technologies that are getting into this business.

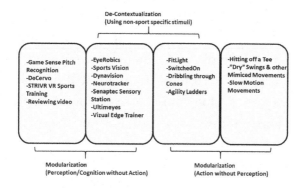

Figure 3.4 - Sports Training Technologies and Methods Built on the Traditional Business Model of Producing Movements

Much like the cortical keyboard and computer analogies, the key feature of this business model of skill is that our movements are controlled by a Central Executive: the boss (in our brain) that issues the commands to move and solves the problem of choice for us. Acquiring and improving a skill involves developing the controller's general abilities: perception, attention, anticipation, memory and decision making. The actual execution of the movement is subservient to these higher-level processes. Once a decision is made about what course of action to take, the different components of the motor system (your different body parts, the workers in the factory if you will) become organized because they follow the plan, the GMP, given from on high.

. . .

But there seem to be some fundamental flaws with this business model. First, how do we achieve the all-important adaptability we discussed in Chapter 2? For example, how does Nadal successfully return the ball if, as he claims, every shot is different? Does he have a separate business plan (a GMP) stored in his head for every possible combination of spin, shot direction, speed, opponent, surface, weather condition, etc.? This problem gets even worse when we consider the number of degrees of freedom that need to be specified in each business plan. Returning to our tennis forehand example in Figure 3.1, movement around the shoulder joint involves 10 muscles, movement around the elbow involves six, there are four muscles that move your forearm (the radio-ulnar joint), and six muscles that rotate the wrist. If we add all that all up, that is 26 different parameters that must be specified for each of the possible combinations of internal and external conditions Nadal described. We better have one heck of a data storage room in our movement control business!

It is also the case that research examining sports training programs built on this traditional business model (including some of those in Figure 3.4) has demonstrated that they are not very effective. In particular, there is no real evidence that pulling apart abilities like perception and decision making, training them out of context and then back together will actually transfer to improved performance in the overall skill you were trying to improve in the first place[2][3].

For example, in 2019 Formenti and colleagues[4] studied the effects of training on a system called Neurotracker for improving volleyball performance. Neurotracker basically involves playing a virtual shell game in which you are asked to follow a small set of yellow spheres that move randomly around on a computer screen. Your job is to keep track of a small set of the spheres and pick them out at the end when the movement stops. This training is modular – we are trying to improve perception and attention separately from acting as there is no movement involved other than clicking on the screen at the end. It is also context independent – the players are looking at abstract, unmeaningful objects, not volleyballs that were served at them or opponents on the other team.

What was found in this study? After training, the volleyball players were much better at doing the Neurotracker task but there was absolutely no improvement in setting, passing or serving accuracy on the court as compared to a control group. There was no *transfer of training*. This general pattern is what has been found across a wide range of general "brain training" tools that attempt to develop general perceptual-cognitive abilities out of context (for example, phone apps like Lumosity.) The findings to support this type of training are so unconvincing that the FTC has even stepped in a couple times with large fines to companies for making unsupported claims[5] [6]

Is there a better, more straight-forward way to solve Bernstein's degrees-of-freedom problem? Don't look now, there is a new company opening up across the street with no boss at all! Introducing "Self-Organization LLC".

The Self-Organization View

To understand the alternative view of how we learn to control our movements, let's compare and contrast two things you might see at your local football field: a marching band and a flock of birds. Both systems involve a set of components that move in a highly coordinated way: the band members march out highly entertaining patterns of movement while the birds dive and swoop together in different directions. But let's think for a second about how the organization arises in each of these cases. The marching band uses our traditional business model of control. The Central Executive (the choreographer) comes up with the action plan and gives specific instructions to each of the band members (when you get to the 50 yard-line turn left, etc.). Organization comes from having a good plan and each member executing it with no errors. The birds, however, have no central controller. There is no leader bird in a flock that is telling all the other birds which direction to turn and when. There is no avian choreographer. How is it possible for there to be order and organization if leadership does not impose it from above?

The incredible feats of high speed and precise coordination we see in a flock of birds are so astounding that they have been attributed to some far-fetched mechanisms over the years. Early explanations for flocking included thought transference and electromagnetic communication. A more plausible theory of flocking behavior in birds was proposed by Wayne Potts in 1984[7]. Potts filmed flocking maneuvers made by a species of bird called a Dunlin. The first thing he observed was that the time between when one bird started its turn and the others followed seemed too short to be physically possible. When he startled a bird with a light flash in his lab, their reaction time was about 40 msec. Yet, their time to start a turn in a flock was only about 15 msec. When flocking they were turning faster than they could react. What's going on here? Potts proposed that the birds were essentially forming an avian chorus line. He observed that maneuvers began with a small number of birds (usually only one) turning into flock. This causes the birds closest to it to react and turn away. As this continues, birds further from the original agitator bird see this all occurring and begin to anticipate that they are going to need to turn much in the same way members of a chorus look down the line to anticipate when they are going to have to lift their leg. This anticipation caused a propagation through the flock leading to high (faster than reaction) speed turns we see in the sky.

The business model used by a flock of birds is one of *self-organization*. That is, the order and structure in the company arises from the interactions between the lower-level components of the system, not from some rules or a plan given by a higher level, central controller. The workers are organizing themselves using only the information available to them, without the need for a boss. And as shown by Potts' research on birds, one of the most amazing things about this type of organization is that patterns can emerge from these local interactions between the workers that are totally unexpected. Self-organization is seen throughout nature from structure formation in cells, to patterns formed in inanimate objects like sand, to the schooling of fish.

Our new business model also has some fundamental differences in terms of structure and process. The business organizational chart is now what is shown in Figure 3.5. Instead of having a hierarchical system led by the Central Executive we have perception-action coupling. That is, our actions are directly controlled by what we perceive (without any need for processing and analysis). When we act it changes the information coming in from our perceptual systems. And through this, "decisions" emerge. Think again about the flock of birds. A bird in a flock does not turn because it is given an instruction to do so. Nor does it really make an explicit decision: "I need to turn now". Flying in a flock requires the bird to continuously adjust its movements based on perceptual information about how close its neighbors are. When the agitator bird in Potts' study turned back into the flock, this information would tell its nearest neighbor bird "it's getting too close" so they would turn away. The decision was part and parcel with what it was already doing in controlling its flight. Perceiving, acting and deciding are all working together in one big department.

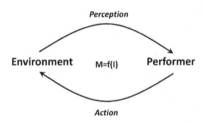

Figure 3.5 - Perception-action coupling. Movement (M) is a function of information (I) from the environment.

The self-organization business model has some very different implications for training. Because there is not a linear flow of separable processes involved, they can't be broken out into modules, pulled apart to train, and then put back together. In a self-organizing system, the "business plan" comes from often unpredictable interactions between the workers. So, they need to all be there in training. Furthermore, context is everything! A bird in a flock doesn't need to just perceive any old type of movement – to be a part of the chorus line they need to detect the specific pattern of movement which tells them when and how they need to act. Remember in Potts' study he found the birds moved completely differently when presented with an abstract, out of context signal (a flash of light) as compared to the real information (another bird coming towards them). Success in this business relies on working groups (often called "soft assemblies") temporarily assigned to the immediate, specific action problem we need to solve, rather than permanent, general departments that try to solve all problems.

What are the advantages of solving Bernstein's degrees of freedom problem via a self-organization business model? Well first, it provides a much more effective way to handle the internal and external variability we must deal with when performing an action. If we can form temporary working groups of components that will interact to solve a specific movement problem, we are much more readily adaptable to changing conditions. Think again about the flock of birds. They can be successful in a multitude of different situations: agitator bird turns in different directions or speeds, different number of birds in the flock, wind coming from different directions, etc. A self-organizing system adapts to all these variations just through the local interactions between the birds. We do not need to come up with executive level plans for every possible situation we might face.

The second big advantage is that a self-organizing business is much more robust to "errors" made by one of the workers. What happens in a marching band when one of the members turns the wrong way? As you might imagine the outcome is not good and there are several examples of blooper videos you can find on YouTube showing it. In a system controlled by a plan given from a central executive this is not at all surprising. All the cymbals player has been told is that they are supposed to turn left when they get to the 50-yard line. They have been given no instruction about what to do if the trombone player is suddenly coming towards them. For a self-organizing system this is not a problem because each component is controlling their action based on information in the moment. A flocking bird does not "turn right when you get above that tree". It turns to keep a safe distance from its neighbor in a manner that depends on how their neighbor turns. This is why flocking birds often seem to swerve and change direction suddenly. If one bird makes a "mistake" and turns in the wrong direction, the other birds adjust and self-organize into another pattern.

So, we don't need a boss! We can have order and organization in a system like the human body without the requirement of the Central Executive controlling everything above. Furthermore, a self-organizing system seems to be much better prepared to produce the variability in movement we need to handle the ever-changing environment conditions we act in. But what guides this process of self-organization? If we are a coach or trainer, do we have to just stand back and let the performer do everything themselves? Or can we influence this self-organization process in some way?

4

FREEDOM THROUGH CONSTRAINTS?!

Think about a soccer match played by young children. Can you see the ball? It is in there somewhere amongst the cloud of players all moving around the field together. Here we have a system that tends to self-organize into a very amusing but ineffective pattern. When faced with all the different action possibilities - moving into open space, driving for the opponent's net, passing to different teammates, shooting, etc. - almost all of the players just choose to do the same thing: "go for the ball". If this was our flock of birds, we would have a real mess to clean up! If we are not going to be a boss and tell each player what they should be doing (and instead allow for self-organization), how do we get the young soccer players to better coordinate their movements? The answer to the problem of too much choice, Bernstein's degrees of freedom problem, would seem to be an obvious one: take away some options. But, as we will see, the results it produces are quite surprising.

．　．　．

To understand this more let's travel to Brazil, a country known for superior self-organization in soccer. Despite incredible success in producing top-level players, many areas of Brazil do not have the top-level training facilities that can be found in other countries. Instead, for many young players (including most famously, Pele) a large proportion of practice occurs via a customary pickup game called 'pelada'[1]. The term, which can be translated from Portuguese as "nude", captures that fact that it is typically played in a naked environment absent of proper grass fields, nets, line markers or coaches. It usually played outdoors on very irregular surfaces including dirt streets and sandy beaches. They base team structure on who shows up that day: the number of players on each team is often much less than on a typical soccer side and there are no structured leagues as players of both sexes and all ages typically play together.

Figure 4.1 - Brazilian Pelada

On the surface, it would seem having to resort to the highly unstructured practice conditions in pelada should put Brazilian players at a significant disadvantage as compared to those in other countries. If training in Brazil is naked, the emperor in England and many European countries like Germany, Spain,

Portugal and the Netherlands is fully clothed! In these countries, the dominant model for developing players over the past 50 years or so has been the youth soccer academy. In these academies, players (as young as nine years of age) are signed to a contract with a professional team. They are then given a formalized training program (including specific drills to work on outside of training and a nutrition program), access to world class training facilities and coaches, specialist training for different positions and participate in weekly matches organized by age group. How is it possible that Brazil can compete with these highly formalized systems and be known for developing some of the most skilled players in the world? Is it possible that that somehow the "disadvantages" of pelada are advantageous? Before we address this question, let's look at another curious example of the benefits of playing around in sand.

Arm injuries in baseball pitchers have become an epidemic[2]. Having to get Tommy John or TJ surgery, which involves replacing the torn Ulnar Collateral Ligament (UCL) in a pitcher's elbow with a ligament from another part of the body, seems to be a question of when not if for baseball pitchers. If you sit down to watch a Major League Baseball (MLB) game, there is roughly an 85% chance you will see a pitcher who has had TJ surgery! While there are many causes of pitcher injuries, one of the key factors that has been identified is the major emphasis placed on increasing pitch velocity. Trying to throw as hard as possible often leads to pitchers to use a throwing technique that concentrates extreme amounts of force on parts of the body, dramatically increasing the chance of injury. To achieve the short-term gain of increased velocity, the athlete is essentially overriding the body's long term injury protection mechanisms, including the variability one we discussed in Chapter 2.

. . .

An example of this is when a pitcher does not land square on their front foot and instead rolls their ankle slightly. This makes the front foot position highly unstable leading to pressure on the ankle, knee and elbow that increases the risk of injury. How might we address this in training? For a group of coaches on the Dutch National Baseball team, the answer involves taking the clothes off the training environment. That is, moving the pitcher from a nicely manicured mound to a sand pit not unlike the beaches of Brazil – well its likely a bit colder! Having them pitch in uneven, soft sand[3]. How is it possible that these seemingly non-optimal training conditions serve to lead to highly effective self-organization of skill? To understand what is going on we need to consider the *constraints* imposed on the athletes in these cases...

Newell's Constraints Model of Coordination

What if I told you that one of the single most influential publications in sports coaching today is not about sports or coaching at all - It is a book chapter about motor development in children. In 1986, Karl Newell was trying to put forth a different view to the traditional thinking about how kids develop motor skills[4]. Specifically, he sought to counter the dominant idea at the time that our genes carry prescriptions for actions that emerge at different times or critical periods. Newell argued that our movements were not prescribed by anything, there is no CEO in our head – instead as we grow and develop, movements emerge as results of a self-organization process that is bound by the ever-changing constraints imposed upon us. So, there is that magic word: constraint. What exactly does it mean?

. . .

A constraint is something that eliminates certain possibilities or options for action. Keeping with my microwave example – it removes some of the buttons. So key point number one, actions are not caused by constraints. When a new constraint is added it is not prescribing a particular action from a performer. Rather, constraints serve to exclude some actions. So, the performer still comes up with their own movement solution through self-organization – it's just that their potential options for doing this have been reduced or constrained. In Bernstein's terminology, we have reduced the number of degrees of freedom.

As illustrated in the now iconic "constraints triangle" shown in Figure 4.2, Newell proposed that there are three different types of constraints that serve to shape our movement: individual, environmental, and task. Individual (aka organismic) constraints are things you and I bring to the table when we perform a skill. These include physical properties including our height, weight, strength, speed, flexibility, etc. Think about the example of playing tennis from last chapter. It goes without saying that Rafael Nadal walks on to the court with very different individual constraints than you or me. In particular, his lateral movement speed and acceleration are likely much higher. What does this do to his pattern of coordination? When a ball is played to his backhand, he has the choice of playing the backhand or "running around the ball" to play a forehand. Because you and I are slower, the latter option is not available to us – constraints change the movement solutions available to us.

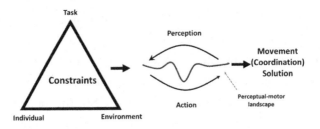

Figure 4.2 - Newell's Constraints Model

Environmental constraints are general properties of the world around us like gravity, wind, temperature, the slipperiness of the surface we are playing on, light level, etc. For the most part, these types of constraints will have an effect no matter what type of skill we are trying to perform. Imagine walking to park where you see a group of people playing baseball, another group playing soccer and another playing tennis. If the wind picked up, it starts to get dark, or the sprinklers broke and flooded the park, it is going to affect all these activities. Of course, in most cases, a coach will not have any control over the environmental constraints during practice. But, as I will discuss in Chapter 7, they are still something that can be taken advantage of, so maybe don't cancel that training session because the field is a bit wet or it is windy out.

The final type of constraints are the ones we are going to be looking at most in this book because they are the ones that a coach or trainer has the greatest control over. Task constraints are factors that are highly specific to the skill being performed. Consider my example of groups playing baseball, soccer and tennis in a park. If I told the baseball players that they were only allowed to pitch underhand it would have no effect on the soccer or tennis players. If I gave the tennis players shorter racquets and smaller tennis balls it would have no effect on the baseball or soccer players. Finally, if I told the soccer players that they could only have three players on each team it would not affect baseball or tennis. As these examples illustrate, task constraints include things like the rules of the game, the equipment being used, and the number and spacing of players on a field.

With the knowledge of Newell's constraints triangle in hand, let's consider the different ways constraints can shape how we learn to move...

Constraining to simplify the degrees of freedom problem

The most fundamental role constraints play in learning a new skill is helping us solve the problem of choice – Bernstein's degrees of freedom problem. Think about learning to serve a volleyball. How much should you rotate your shoulder? Bend your elbow? Flex your wrist? Should you try a jump serve and which requires figuring out what you are going to do with your ankles, knees and hips too?! If our perceptual-motor system were completely unconstrained there would literally be an infinite number of different ways we could serve the ball. How do we decide what to do? The answer is we add some constraints.

Not to be one to leave his own problem's unsolved, Bernstein proposed that when we first learn a new movement skill, we constraint ourselves naturally through a process he called *freezing* degrees of freedom. As illustrated in Figure 4.3 and 4.4, there are

49

two ways he proposed that this would occur. The first involves rigidly, fixing separate degrees of freedom by not using particular joints or muscles during movement. Simply put, if you can't figure out how much you should bend your elbow when serving a tennis ball, then don't! By keeping that joint locked and straight you are removing it as a degree of freedom and simplifying the self-organization process. The second type of freezing proposed by Bernstein was introducing strong, temporary couplings between degrees of freedom. So instead of just keeping a particular body part (like my elbow) rigid and locked, I can couple its movement to another body part, so they move together. For example, I could make it so my elbow and shoulder rotate at the same rate. By adding the constraint that these two body parts move together, in-sync I have again simplified the degrees of freedom problem – in this case, by using one motor command to cover two different joints. In Chapter 9, we will look at some examples of freezing in different sports and we also see why this is not the best way to solve the degrees of freedom problem.

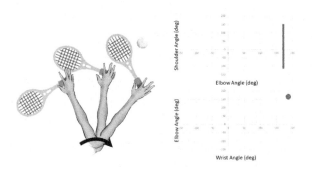

Figure 4.3 – Freezing Type I. The performer is simplifying the problem of coordinating degrees of freedom for a tennis stroke but not using any rotation around the elbow or wrist joints.

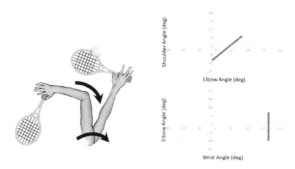

Figure 4.4 – Freezing Type II. The performer is simplifying the degrees of freedom problem for a tennis stoke by establishing a rigid coupling between the shoulder and elbow joints in which they both rotate at the same rate and time.

Beyond freezing, there are multiple ways a coach can manipulate constraints to help reduce the degrees of freedom problem and make self-organization more effective. Returning to the example I used to start this chapter, a coach giving players on a soccer field instructional constraints ("you are the left winger so stay on the left side of the field", "you are playing defense so stay back near our goal") quickly serves to prevent all players swarming around the ball.

Constraining to amplify errors and take away ineffective movement solutions

Another way that constraints can be manipulated to help the business of self-organization is by taking away movement solutions that a coach or therapist has identified as being sub-optimal or potentially injury-causing. A great example of this can be seen in the baseball pitching example I described earlier.

Moving a pitcher that does not land square on their lead foot from a practice field with firm grass to soft sand is a change in an environmental constraint. It helps by making the problem we are trying to get rid of worse! When you roll your ankle slightly when landing on firm ground it creates a slight imbalance our system will tolerate. When you do the same on a soft surface it makes the roll much larger and can make the pitcher almost fall over. By changing constraints, we have made the movement solution the performer is currently using ineffective and have encouraged them to find a new one.

This type of constraints manipulation is sometimes called the *Method of Amplification of Errors* because it is taking a slight "flaw" in a movement pattern and making it much larger and louder to the perceptual system of the performer. Another example can be seen in the study of golfers by Milanese and colleagues[5]. Using a motion capture system, the researchers identified a particular error in the golf swing of 34 participants: not shifting their weight away from the ball onto their back foot while swinging. This is problematic because weight transfer serves to generate force and consequently distance on the shot. The golfers were then split into two training groups. The corrective instruction group were given the traditional type of coaching one would expect, specifically they were told to "Shift your body weight toward the BACK FOOT as far as possible while swinging". In other words, they were told the solution to the problem. The error amplification group were given a very odd instruction: "Shift your body weight toward the FRONT FOOT as far as possible while swinging". So, in other words, they were told to make the problem even worse. What was found? For the error amplification group, both club head and ball speed increased after training (what we would expect if weight is being transferred more effectively from the front to the back foot) while there was no significant improvement for either the direct instruction or a control group that received no training. So, counterintuitively, adding a constraint that exaggerates or amplifies a problem in a movement solution rather than trying to give the athlete the solution to correct it seems to be more effective. Other commonly used examples of this type of training involve using a task constraint manipulation by changing equipment. For example, using a flexible shaft golf club or a PVC pipe instead of a baseball bat can serve to amplifying any "hitches" (i.e., unsmooth transfers of force) in a golfers or baseball player's swing.

Creating opportunities for action by changing constraints

So far, we have looked at ways constraints can be used to take possible movement solutions away from a performer. But they can also be used to create new ones. One way that we can do this is through appropriate manipulation of the task constraints of equipment. Think about a young child trying to learn to play basketball on a standard 10 foot basketball hoop. The problem here is not so much one of too much choice but rather not enough options due to the mismatch between the task constraint and the action capacity of the player. In order to get the ball 10 feet high most young players will need to put their whole body into shot. This situation creates a couple different problems. First, there is a very low success rate, so the child becomes discouraged and loses motivation to keep practicing. Second, it is not an effective way to learn the movement pattern associated with an effective jump shot. As Chase and colleagues[6] have shown, reducing a basketball rim to 8 feet height serves to both increase the number of shots made and the associated feelings self-efficacy (the belief in one's ability to succeed in achieving a goal) in the child.

A similar situation can be seen in tennis where children are typically asked to play with large adult racquets and bouncy, high compression balls. In a wonderful series of studies by Tim Buszard and colleagues (which I will be diving into in detail in Chapter 11), it has been shown that while using adult tennis equipment leads to a flat swing and strike the ball close to the body, switching the task constraint to a smaller racquet and lower compression ball results in a low to high swing path and the ball being struck out in front. Both these changes in the movement solution result in a more powerful and accurate forehand.

The other main way constraints can be manipulated to create action opportunities for a performer is by changing their individual constraints through appropriate strength and conditioning training. An example of the potential of this can be seen in the work on soccer goalkeeping by Matt Dicks and colleagues[7]. When attempting to save a penalty kick in soccer, a goalkeeper is faced with conflicting objectives. They must start their dive early enough to be able to cover the distance between where they are standing and the corner of the net before they ball gets there. But they also need to wait long enough before starting their dive to get information from the shooter about the direction the shot is going. Before asking them try to stop kicks, Dicks et al measured the individual constraints of each of the goalkeepers. Specifically, their movement time or how long it took them to get from standing still in the middle of the goal to reaching the corner. They found that the goalkeepers with quicker movement times consistently waited a bit longer before starting their dive and subsequently got more information about where the shot was going. And, not surprisingly, they stopped more kicks. Having greater action capacity (or a different individual constraint of movement time) gave the quicker goalkeeper options for a movement solution that was not available to slower keepers. Thus, improving this individual constraint of movement time through training (and thus increasing their available movement solutions) could be a way to allow soccer goalkeepers to better self-organize. And, as we will see next chapter, it is also likely to completely change the way they perceive the world.

Constraining to create variability and essential noise

The final way that constraints can be manipulated to aid self-organization and skill acquisition is introducing variability and some of that essential noise we looked at in Chapter 2. Remember that in this new view of learning our goal is not to develop one ideal technique that we can repeat over and over. Instead, we want to be adaptable and flexible so that we can use different movement solutions to achieve our goal in the face of ever-changing conditions. In Bernstein's words, we want to have *dexterity* in our movement:

"Dexterity is the ability to find a motor solution for any external situation, that is, to adequately solve any emerging motor problem"

Moving skillfully involves coming up with new solutions to new problems not just repeating the same old solution. How do we learn to solve problems? By practicing a lot of different ones. In other words, by having variability in our practice conditions.

· · ·

An example of manipulating task constraints to add variability can be seen in one of my own studies that I like to refer to as my labor of love – because it took 10 years to complete! In this study, I used a baseball batting virtual reality (VR) environment to train high school baseball players[8]. The VR environment was comprised of a large screen with the image of the pitcher, ball and field. The batter swung a real bat (equipped with a motion tracker) at the virtual approaching ball and the computer software calculated whether bat-ball contact occurred. If it did, the ball flew out on the virtual field (in the appropriate direction and distance based on the calculations), the batter heard a sound and the bat vibrated. The type of sound ("thud" vs "crack of the bat") and the amount of vibration (strong vs weak) depended on how close the point of contact was to the bat's sweet spot. My motivation for using this environment for training was to address a problem I saw with traditional batting practice: low variability in conditions. When hitting off a pitching machine in practice, typically the settings on the machine are not changed from pitch to pitch. That is, the type of pitch (fastball vs curveball), speed and location are the same every time. How can a batter become a dexterous, adaptable problem solver when they are always solving the same problem?

In my study, I compared four training groups. Two of the groups just received extra, traditional batting practice (on top of their regular team practice) in which the pitch parameters were the same for every pitch in a training session. One of the groups (Real BP) did this on the field against a pitching machine while the other (Virtual BP) did the same but in the VR environment. The third group was the necessary control group that did no extra training outside of their regular practice. The fourth group was the one I was most excited about. For this group, I took advantage of the VR environment to add variability to practice by changing the task constraints. Specifically, the speed, type and locations of the pitch were changed based on how well the batter was performing. If you made contact on two 85 mph pitches in a row, the next one was 87 mph. If you hit two fastballs in a row, I threw in a curveball. If you could hit pitches that varied in their height they crossed the plate by 1 foot, I increased the variation to 2 feet. In other words, batters in this group were given lots and lots of problems to solve! After six weeks of training, all batters completed both real and virtual batting tests, and I recorded their league statistics from their final (senior) year of competition. What made the study take so long was that after all this was completed, I just sat on the results and waited for five years to see where each player ended up. Did the go to play in college? Were they drafted by an MLB team? Or was high school the last time they played competitive baseball.

The results (which I finally published in 2017) are shown in Figure 4.5. Manipulating the task constraints of pitch type, speed and location to add more variability to the practice conditions had profound effects on hitting ability. Batters in the high variability group did significantly better on all hitting tests, had a higher on base percentage (a statistic which takes into account getting on base via a hit or a walk) in their senior session, and a significantly greater proportion went to play higher levels of baseball. In Chapter 9, I will look in more detail at why these effects occurred by digging into the actual mechanics of the swing. But suffice it to say for now, variability in practice leads to more adaptable problems solvers.

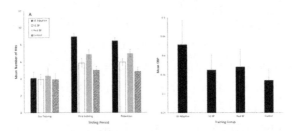

Figure 4.5 – Results from my study using VR to manipulate constraints in baseball batting training. Reproduced with permission from Gray, R. (2017). Transfer of training from virtual to real baseball batting. Frontiers in Psychology.

And this takes us back to the streets and beaches of Brazil. Playing pelada essentially achieves the same thing as my baseball VR environment. Playing on rough or sandy surfaces adds variability to the movement of the ball under one's feet pushing the perceptual-motor system to adapt. Playing with different numbers of players changes the space available on the field for shooting and passing the ball. Playing against opponents of different ages and sizes alters one's ability to win the ball or drive past an opponent with strength. As first purposed by Uehera and colleagues[9], the presumed "disadvantage" of having to play pelada instead of practicing at a youth academy facility may be a distinct advantage for Brazilian soccer players because they play under a wider range of task constraints.

Constraints and the Emergence of Movement Solutions

We will look at many more examples of constraints throughout the book but just a few key points to emphasize. Unlike the prescriptive way movement skills have traditionally been coached, the manipulation of constraints is not an attempt to give the performer the solution (the "correct" technique) to the problem. At no time in my baseball study did I give batters any feedback or instruction about how to swing. Nary a coach can be found at a game of pelada. And, in perhaps the most extreme example, the coaching instruction used in the error amplification golf study told golfers exactly what not to do! I like to think of constraints as informative boundaries. They guide self-organization by pushing performers away from certain solutions, encouraging them to look for others, and providing them information about how they should change how they are moving. This latter effect is why error amplification works – it allows the performer to figure out on their own why they pattern of coordination they are currently using is not effective. Instead of movement techniques being drilled into an athlete through repetition, in this new view of learning, skill *emerges* in the face of the constraints involved. Finally, we saw that the process of self-organization (and learning a new skill) depends on the individual constraints (physical traits and action capacities) each of us brings to the table. Next, we will see that these constraints not only influence how we move and act they also change how we perceive the world around us.

5

WE PERCEIVE THE WORLD IN TERMS OF
WHAT OUR BODY AFFORDS US

I n parallel to the anti-repetition revolution which has changed the way we think about how we move in our environment, there has been an equally revolutionary sea change in our understanding of how we *perceive* it. Look around you right now. What is your visual system trying to achieve? The traditional assumption has been that it is trying to accurately register the physical properties of the world around you. How far away are things? How big are they? How fast are they moving? These inputs are then used to create a multi-purpose representation of our environment that we can use for controlling our actions. So, the goal of perception is to break the world down into the variables we learned about in physics class (distance, size, speed, slant, etc.), reconstruct what is out there and then pass this information along to the motor control department in our hierarchical business model from Chapter 3. In this view, what we perceive should depend exclusively on the layout on the environment around us. If the distances, sizes and speeds of the objects around us stays the same from one event to next then we should perceive the same thing, right?

. . .

But let's consider for a second some comments athletes have made about how they perceive their world[1]. After hitting a 500 ft home run, Mickey Mantle once famously said, 'I just saw the ball as big as a grapefruit'. The somewhat less accomplished Joe 'Ducky' Medwick once claimed that being in a slump in baseball was like "swinging at aspirins". In commenting on playing at a championship level, tennis player John McEnroe claimed, "Things slow down, the ball seems a lot bigger and you feel like you have more time". Basketball player Dennis Scott said that on good nights making his shots was "like throwing a pebble in the ocean". While we need to treat subjective impressions like this with some caution, there seems to be a common theme here: the perception of the world is changing depending on our ability to act on it! When an athlete is more capable and performing well objects like a baseball, tennis ball or a basketball hoop look bigger. When they are struggling, they look smaller. How is this possible if our perceptual system is trying to accurately represent the physical layout of our environment and the environment is not changing?

The answer is that the perception of our environment is not solely based on its physical properties. Instead, perception is *embodied*. That is, the information we detect about the sizes, distances and speeds of objects is scaled by our ability to act on these objects. The perceived steepness of a hill facing a cyclist is determined both by the slope of the surface projected on their eye and by their level of fatigue. The perceived size of a golf hole is related to both its size and the precision with which the performer can putt the ball. This embodied perception approach to perception argues that what we perceive is not a true representation of 'what is out there' but rather reflects our ability to act on objects in our environment. Changes in our action capacity (think the individual constraints from Chapter 4) change our perception. Before we consider why and how this might occur, let's look at few more examples.

Some of the most interesting work on embodied perception comes from studies that have looked at people's ability to judge the slope or slant of a surface. When standing at the bottom of a hill or set of stairs that need to be climbed people judge the identical hill or stairs to be steeper when you ask them to wear a heavy backpack full of books[2]. People that are shorter, older or heavier perceive the slant to be steeper than those that are taller, younger or lighter. In a clever study, Taylor-Covill and Eves[3] stopped people at the bottom of a flight of stairs in a subway terminal and offered them a choice between water and a sugary, energy drink. The individuals that choose the energy drink judged the flight of stairs to be steeper, on average. Again, we see action capacity is influencing perception. Having more weight to carry (either due to a heavy load or your own body), having to take more strides to get up a flight of stairs (due to short legs), or being energy depleted (which presumably motivates you to choose an energy drink over water) all make a slope you need to climb look steeper.

Turning back to world of sports, there have been several studies that provide support for the observations by Mantle, McEnroe and the like[4]. Athletes performing at a higher level (as measured by game statistics) judge baseballs, football uprights, the bullseye on a dartboard, archery targets, tennis balls, and golf holes to be bigger as compared to their lesser skilled counterparts. Making a sports task more difficult by giving a player a smaller racquet, putt from a longer distance, or try to hit the ball to a particular location on the field (e.g., to the opposite field in baseball) leads to the balls and holes looking smaller. Golfers that "choke" under pressure perceive the hole as getting smaller while those that are "clutch" do not[5].

Why do we perceive the world in this odd, embodied way? Wouldn't it be better to just try to accurately represent what is out there? What possible function could it serve? For the answers to the questions, let's bring in another one of the central figures in our skill revolution...

Gibson's Affordances

James J (or JJ) Gibson was appointed a Professor at Cornell University in 1950. During his time there as a researcher and teacher, which continued until his passing in 1979, he methodically developed a theory of perception that would culminate in a set of seminal books that I can see sitting worn out and dog eared on my shelf as I type: *The Perception of the Visual World, The Sense Considered as Perceptual Systems* and *The Ecological Approach to Visual Perception.* But I would also like to highlight an earlier part of his career that has a striking parallel to Bernstein's. In 1941, Gibson entered the U.S. Army, where he became the director of a unit for the Army Air Forces' Aviation Psychology Program during World War II. Of course, of particular interest to him, was the effect flying an aircraft had on visual perception, and how we might be able to develop visual aptitude tests for screening out pilot applicants. Just as was the case with Bernstein, Gibson's thinking was shaped by having to address, real-world applied problems. So, what exactly were Gibson's ideas about perception and how do they differ from conventional views?

First, let's return to the idea (that was dominant during Gibson's time) that our perceptual system is not embodied but instead is just trying to accurately represent the physical properties of the outside world. Imagine you are a baseball outfielder running to catch a fly ball and your visual system detects the ball's physical properties to let you know that it will land 10 feet from where you are now in 2 seconds. What should you do with this knowledge? Keep running at the same speed? Slow down and play the ball on a bounce? Dive? How do we get from distance and time (perceptual information) to running and catching (action)? If our perceptual system's primary job is to pick up information about the physical properties of the world like size, speed, time and distance we would be stuck be because such properties have no meaning to our body (the motor control department) in and of themselves.

The traditional view is that meaning in situations like this comes from knowledge stored in our brain. For example, an experienced baseball player could have a store of memory of different plays. She/he could then match the current situation to a memory to know what to do – when the ball is that far away, diving allowed me to catch it in the past. Or, alternatively, could have stored in their brain a set of if X then Y rules learned from a coach. If the ball is hit here, I do this. Like the business model we discussed in Chapter 3, perception is given meaning from the top – the executive controller in our brain.

. . .

So, what exactly was Gibson's alternative account of adding meaning to the perception of our environment? It is quite simple, really. Gibson first noted that, in our environment, surfaces *afford* (that is they provide or supply) opportunities for action. Flat surfaces provide opportunities to rest, surfaces with gaps provide opportunities to pass through, hanging surfaces provide opportunities to seek shelter, and so. Furthermore, there is information in the structure of light, sound, touch, etc. which directly specifies the qualities of these surfaces. Light reflects differently off flat, gapped and hanging surfaces. Given these two things it is possible that what we perceive is what a surface affords (or in other words, what we can or cannot do with it) rather than just action neutral properties like their distance, size, etc. In Gibson's words:

"How do we go from surfaces to affordances? And if there is information in light for the perception of surfaces, is there information for the perception of what they afford? Perhaps the composition and layout of surfaces constitute what they afford. If so, to perceive them is to perceive what they afford. This is a radical hypothesis, for it implies that the "values" and "meanings" of things in the environment can be directly perceived". [6]

Perceiving affordances is to carve the world up in meaningful units of action rather than using the meaningless units of physics. In Gibson's words:

"The perceiving of an affordance is not a process of perceiving a value-free physical object to which meaning is somehow added in a way that no one has been able to agree upon; it is a process of perceiving a value-rich ecological object. Any substance, any surface, any layout has some affordance for benefit or injury to someone. Physics may be value-free, but ecology is not".

For a performer, gaps do not look wide, opponents don't look near, and pitches don't look fast. Instead, performers see *pass-through-ability* in a gap, *tackle-ablity* of an opponent and *hit-ability* of a pitch. Perception of opportunities for action not just physical properties. This, in turn, is why the perception changes based on an athlete's ability and the difficulty of a task. When I am struggling at the plate, balls look less hittable even thought their physical size has not changed. When you ask me to carry more weight, the same hill affords less opportunity for climb-ability. When there is the pressure to win a tournament, for some golfers this can change the affordance of sink-ability provided by a golf hole that is always the same physical size. When we ask people to make judgements about the physical world, they tell us about what the world affords to them in terms of opportunities for action not about its "true" physical properties.

So far, we have talked about how we perceive opportunities for action, affordances, from our environment. However, it is obviously the case, that affordances are not the same for everyone – we need to somehow take account of the action capabilities of the perceiver. For example, a baseball pitched at 95 mph that affords hitting for a player with a high bat speed may not have the same affordance for someone with a lower bat speed. Or a regulation sized soccer ball may afford kicking and dribbling for adult but not for a young child. As Gibson put it: "Affordances have to be measured *relative to the animal*. They are unique for that animal. They are not just abstract physical properties. They have unity relative to the posture and behavior of the animal being considered".

Body & Action Capacity Scaling

When we pick up information from the world, we need to somehow incorporate our own action capacities. In most cases, this would not seem to be that much of a challenge. Imagine for a second you are navigating your way through a basement with lots of gaps and spaces trying to find your fuse box. The main affordance you will be picking up is "pass-through-ability". Can I fit through that gap between beams? Can I do it by just walking normally or do I need to rotate my body and go through it sideways? The answer to these questions (what your basement affords you in terms of action opportunity) depends, of course, on your body width. Through experience walking around we would expect that people detect this affordance accurately and indeed that is what research has shown. Take one adult with broad shoulders and one with narrow shoulders and ask them to walk through gaps getting smaller and smaller. As shown in Figure 5.1 (left panel) from a study by Warren & Wang[7], the wider (large) person starts rotating their shoulders to walk through for larger gaps (about 65 cm) that the narrower (small) person walks straight through. If you then take the width of the gap or aperture (A) and divide it by the width of each person's shoulders (S), as shown in the right panel of Figure 5.1, you see that, despite the large difference in physical size, both people are doing the same thing – they are rotating their shoulders when the gap no long affords "pass-through-ability" by walking normally, for them. Their perception of the size of the aperture is perfectly scaled to the width of shoulders. Or, stated another way, our perception is well calibrated to our action capacity. Another example can be seen when people are asked to judge whether stairs with different riser heights are climbable or not. No matter whether a person is 5 foot or 7 feet tall, they will all tell you that a step with a riser height that is roughly ¼ of the length of their leg affords the best climbing[8]. Again, we carve up the world into pieces that are meaningful FOR US not just perceive its value-free physical properties.

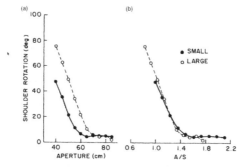

Figure 6. Mean maximum shoulder rotation when walking through an aperture as a function of (A) aperture width and (B) the ratio of aperture width to shoulder width, for small and large participants (from Warren & Whang, 1987, with permission).

Figure 5.1 – Affordances of "pass-through-ability"
of a gap. From Warren & Wang (1987)

Ok, so we can perceive the world in terms of our body dimensions. Big deal! How, hard is that really? For most of us, things like our height, shoulder width and leg length are not going to change any time soon. But what if this was not the case? What if your body dimensions systematically changed over a period of a few months? Would you be able to adjust your perception of the world so that you don't bump into things all the time? One of my all-time favorite research studies shows us that the answer is "yes". In an incredibly clever study, Franchak & Adolph[9] investigated the ability of pregnant women to perceive whether doorways of different sizes afforded "squeeze-through-ability". Think about the challenge this poses. Along with all the other things a pregnant woman must deal with there is the problem of re-scaling or re-calibration. A door that afforded passing through in the first trimester may no longer in the third. Amazingly, our perceptual-motor system can seem to handle this no problem. As shown in Figure 5.2, the judgement of whether a door affords "squeeze-through-ability" for pregnant women changes during the course of pregnancy and the change is almost perfectly related to the changes that are occur in their stomach size.

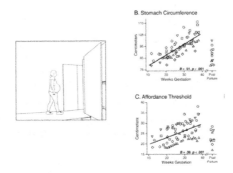

Figure 5.2 – Change in the affordance of "passthrough-ability" during pregnancy. From Franchak & Adolph (2014).

Relating our perception of the world to our action capacities (this amazing calibration process) seems to be a dynamic, ongoing process. And, if you think about it – it must be. As we grow, our physical dimensions change, as we get fatigued or injured our capacity to move changes, and as we train things like our strength, speed and flexibility change. We saw an example of this training effect last chapter: the faster movement times gained through practice afford experienced soccer goalkeepers the opportunity to wait longer to initiate a dive. Let's look at other examples of how practicing a sport changes how we scale our perception of the environment.

In rock climbing, navigating a route up the rock face involves finding areas that afford grasping, called holds. As we have seen, there are two sides to an affordance: the layout of the physical environment (in this case, the surface area of the holds) and the action capacity of the performer (in this case, their grip strength). How does the increased grip strength that comes with practicing rock climbing change one's perception of a rock face? To address this question, van Knobelsdorff and colleagues[10] presented a group of climbers with routes on an indoor rock wall of increasing difficulty (smaller holds and larger distances between holds). To investigate perception, 20 climbers of different skill levels were asked to scan the rock face visually for two minutes and plan their route before climbing. During this time, they wore a portable eye tracking device that allowed the researchers to measure where they look and for how long. What was found? The climbers with relatively weak grip strength used a highly predictable and simple pattern of eye movements when looking at the rock face – they basically just looked at the route with the largest holds. Climbers with greater grip strength showed a much less predictable pattern of gaze, viewing a wide range of possibilities, and took different routes when climbing. Our perception is embodied – our physical capacity is shaping how we view the world. When it is not very large, we see only the limited, predictable opportunities for action. When it is greater, it opens up a new set of affordances for us.

Why is our Perception Embodied?

As Gibson proposed, we seem to perceive our world in this

odd way because it directly supports our ability to act in our environment. Our perceptual system is not designed to gather general-purpose information about the world or try to accurately reconstruct it inside our heads. Its purpose to keep us in contact with action-relevant properties of the specific environment we are acting in. It is directly picking up information to support the selecting of goals, deciding between alternative courses of action and controlling our movements. Let's look at some examples how embodied perception supports us in achieving our goals.

In a study I published in 2013[11], I used my baseball batting VR to look at how a batter's embodied perception supports directional hitting. In baseball, sometimes batters are not just trying to make contact with the ball (which is difficult enough!) they are trying to hit in a particular direction. For example, with a runner on second base and less than two outs in an inning, a batter's goal may be to attempt to hit the ball to right field (even if it results in an "out") so that the base runner can move to third base and be driven home by a sacrifice fly hit by the next batter. A large part of the success in this skill, sometimes called "situational hitting", involves selecting the right pitches to swing at to achieve one's goal. For example, hitting a ball to the "pull field" (e.g., attempting to hit the ball to right field for a batter standing on the right side of the plate, as viewed from behind) is most easily achieved for pitches that cross the plate close to the batter's body (i.e., "inside" pitches), whereas hitting a ball to the "opposite field" is most easily achieved for pitches that cross the plate far from the batter's body (i.e., "outside" pitches).

In my study, I asked batters to perform three different hitting tasks in separate blocks: opposite field hitting, pull hitting, and an unconstrained condition in which they received points for hitting the ball in any location. The twist I added was that they were also asked to make a judgement about the perceived size of the ball – specifically, after each swing they indicated whether the ball looked bigger or smaller than a regulation ball. The now, hopefully not too surprising, results are shown in Figure 5.3. When pull hitting, inside pitches looked big and outside pitches looked small. The reverse occurred when they were trying to hit to the opposite field. Why? Because when I asked about the size of the ball, I was tapping in the perceived affordance of hit-ability. Pitch locations that are more suited to the given hitting task are perceived as more "hit-able" – just like Mickey Mantle's grapefruit!

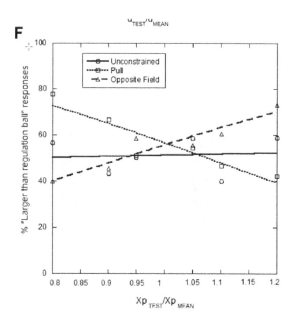

Figure 5.3 – Differences in perceive ball size as a function of the batter's goal. From Gray, R. (2013).

But we are still left with the question: what value does embodied perception have? To address this, I next took advantage of working in VR and altered the size of the simulated balls from pitch-to-pitch. Sometimes they were a bit larger than a normal baseball, sometimes a bit smaller. What I was interested in was the relationship between the size of the ball and how often the batter initiated a swing. The results can be seen in Figure 5.4. When the ball was larger batters swung more often. When it was smaller, they swung less often. So, this seems to be part of the answer. Embodied perception supports *action selection*. When a pitch is more suited for my goal (e.g., an inside pitch for opposite field hitting), I perceive the affordance of "hit-ability", which makes the ball look bigger and makes me more likely to select the action of swinging.

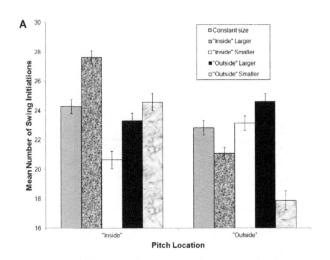

Figure 5.4 – Number of swings for different conditions in which the ball was made larger of small in a baseball batting VR. When the ball was made larger, batters swung more often.

As another example consider the choice shown in the top photo in Figure 5.5. What determines whether we decide to climb a set of stairs or ride an escalator? Eves and colleagues[12] stopped shoppers walking through a mall at the top of the escalator or stairs (i.e., after they had made their choice). They were then asked to judge the slope of the stairs from a photo projected on the wall. On average, the 102 participants that selected the action of climbing the stairs perceived the slope of the stairs to be about 50 deg, while the average for those that selected riding the escalator was nearly 60 deg.

Figure 5.5 – Decisions studied by Taylor-Covill and Eaves. Top: do you go up the stairs or the escalator? Bottom: Do you walk up the nearby stairs or go around and up the ramp in Birmingham City Centre.

Another choice studied by the same researchers can be seen in the bottom photo in Figure 5.5. When walking through the city center of Birmingham, UK you have the choice of climbing a few sets of stairs or walking around on a ramp with a gradual incline. Participants were stopped after they made the choice and asked to judge the perceived slope of the stairs. Again, the 399 people that chose to climb rated the slope to be significantly less than the 370 people that avoided the stairs and went up the ramp. Let's put this all together. People that have less action capacity for climbing stairs because they are carrying something heavier, have shorter legs, or have not eaten enough calories that day, perceive stairs to be steeper. People that perceive stairs to be steeper select actions (e.g., riding an escalator or walking up a ramp) other than climbing. Thus, embodied perception supports an action selection process that helps reduce our energy expenditure and keeps us from becoming overly fatigued.

So, we do not perceive what is out there. The constraints of our environment shape our perception of it in terms of the *task* we are given (e.g., the direction we are asked to hit a ball), the *environment* we act in (e.g., whether we can choose between stairs or an escalator) and is embodied in terms of *individual* constraints (e.g., our leg length or the time required to dive to the corner of a soccer net). And this seems to be highly functional in supporting the control and execution of actions. But let's now turn to the million-dollar question we started all of this with: how do we become skillful? How do the constraints in our environment and the associated embodied perceptions guide us in our search for the optimal way to swing a golf club or position or hands when making a clay pot?

6

LEARNING AS SEARCH, THE LAWS OF ATTRACTION AND THE TIM TEBOW PROBLEM

So, there is no one ideal, correct way to perform a skill, you say? Variability rules the day, you say? Well, then why don't we see completely different movements on every execution of a skill? Why didn't Bernstein's blacksmith swing the hammer overhead on the first swing and underhand on the second? Or two-handed sometimes and one-handed other times? Why do all elite athletes seem to use somewhat similar looking techniques for performing things like jump shots in basketball, chip shots in golf and swings in baseball? If skill really involved this highly variable process of self-organization, shouldn't we see more variety in the way be act? Underhand jump shots, one handed golf shots, or baseball batters that swing with both feet kept together? Why, despite the vast sea of possibilities for ways to move, Bernstein's abundant degrees of freedom, do people performing the same skill seem to converge on similar (but critically, not exactly the same) movement solutions? Despite the increased focus on the role of variability in skillful movement that is not to deny there is not also considerable *invariance* – things that are the same across executions made by the same performer and are similar between different performers.

To understand why this occurs, let's think about learning a new skill as a search through a perceptual-motor landscape like the one illustrated in Figure 6.1. Imagine that you are trying to learn drums and the first task you are given is to play a nice rhythm. The locations in our landscape represent different relationships between what the two drumsticks are doing – technically called their relative phase. These are the possible movement solutions you could use. You begin by hitting both sticks on the drum at the same time –what we call a 0 degrees relative phase relationship or in-phase because both parts of the system are doing the exact same thing. There is 0 separation between them. Well, that is pretty boring! You next start exploring the landscape by trying out other phase relationships. 180 degrees, or anti-phase, where when one stick is contacting the drum, the other is at its peak height. 90 degrees phase - where when one stick is contacting the drum the other is at half its peak height. And so on. We are back to Bernstein's degrees of freedom problem – a seemingly endless number possible different ways you can move. What factors determine where we end up?

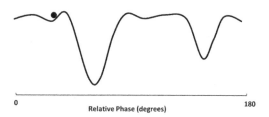

0   180
Relative Phase (degrees)

Figure 6.1 – The perceptual motor landscape

Well, as it turns out, the landscape of perceptual-motor solutions is not flat. Instead, it has a few valleys in it like the ones illustrated in Figure 6.1. As shown in the pioneering work on coordination by Schoner and colleagues[1], when we play the drums there are certain phase relationships that are more attractive and stable than others. That is, they tend to pull us in and once were at that location it is hard to get out. Think of a deep valley in our landscape - once we get near the edge we will slide into it, then we have to climb hard to get back out. You can easily demonstrate this for yourself. Start slowing playing a drum roll (180 degrees anti-phase) with your fingers on the nearest flat surface. Now keep playing faster and faster. Are your fingers still doing opposite things or have they started hitting the surface at the same time? A perfectly in-phase, 0 degrees, phase relationship is a very strong attractor for inter-limb coordination. Even when we do not want to use that movement solution, sometimes we can't help it.

The same kind of effect occurs even when we play at a slower speed. In a study by Zanone and Kelso[2], participants were asked to try to drum using different relative phase relationships, all the way from 0 to 180 degrees. The top panel of Figure 6.2 shows the timing errors produced by most people when doing this. Performance is clearly much, much better at 0 and 180 degrees of relative phase. Why do people have trouble producing a different phase, say 20 degrees? Because they get pulled in and start producing the much more stable 0 degree movement solution, resulting in performance errors. For some reason (we will get to that soon), even though the participants have not been trained at all, 0 and 180 are just more attractive, stable solutions that are easier to execute. But, interestingly, this pattern of results only occurs for about 75% of people. The other 25% exhibit the pattern shown in the bottom panel of Figure 6.2. These people seem to have a 3rd attractor – at 90 deg relative phase.

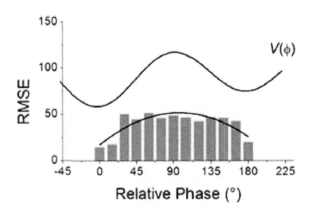

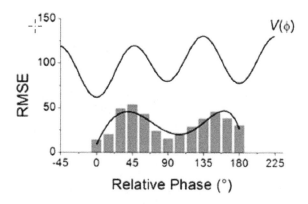

Figure 6.2 – Timing errors when trying to produce different relative phases in drumming. From Kostrubiec et al. (2012).

So, what we are seeing here is that even though, in theory, there are an endless number of movement solutions we could use, we all have certain coordination tendencies. We are attracted to certain solutions that are highly stable and struggle to execute others that are very unstable. We call these tendencies your *intrinsic* (meaning coming from inside) *dynamics* (referring to the motion of our body). And this does not just happen for drumming. There are attractors and intrinsic dynamics for every skill we perform. Figure 6.3a shows the phase relationship between the shin and thigh for a child first learning to walk and for an adult. For adults, there are strong attractors in the movement pattern. For example, almost all adults will have a phase of 0 degrees at about halfway through their stride (50%). Although this pattern is not initially present in the new walker, as shown in Figure 6.3b, the attractors quickly begin to develop within two months of experience walking[3].

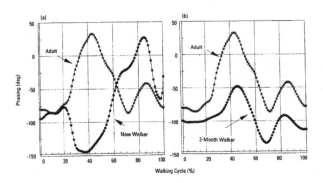

Figure 6.3 – Attractors in walking. From Clark (1995).

Why do these attractors in coordination in exist? Well, as it turns out, they serve some important functions. First, they make us resistant to perturbations. If we step on a stone while walking or a drummer slightly miss hits the drum, although we get initially knocked out of our desired coordination pattern, we will get quickly pulled back into the deep well of the attractor. Second, they help prevent injury and allow us to deal with the extreme time pressures involved in many sporting actions. Think about a basketball player jumping for a rebound then landing back on the ground or possibly on another player's foot. When the player lands, the tendons and muscles in the ankle will send a signal to their brain about the surface, but the transmission of sensory signals is our body is relatively slow. So, there is simply not enough time for it to be used to coordinate the movement of the foot and leg. Instead, we have attractors for coordination or movement that automatically kick in and keep us from getting hurt – well, most of the time, anyways.

In Chapter 2, I made the claim that our body is designed to produce differences and its various systems seem to be built to be inherently noisy and variable. But paradoxically, we see that at the same time it is striving to find stability. Our coordination company, Self Organization LLC, has conflicting mission statements! In order to learn a new skill like drumming, in most cases, we need to get out there and explore the perceptual-motor landscape to find new coordination solutions. We need to be variable in how we move and adapt to the constraints the new task and environment is placing on us. But, at the same time, our individual constraints (and our intrinsic dynamics) are telling us: "no, let's just stay home for the evening and watch a movie. Its comfortable here". Our attractors will resist our attempts to move into less stable regions of landscape. So, how do we satisfy these conflicting goals of exploration and stability?

I'm over you! Breaking free from attractors

These coordination tendencies we all have, while serving some key functions like making us more stable and preventing injury, can also create the "good is the enemy of great" problem for performance. While having attractors at 0 and 180 deg relative phase allows us to get some initial proficiency in pounding out a pattern on the drums, how many songs do you think we could play if we could only produce those relationships? Talk about a boring band!

Another example I like to use is something I have worked on myself for several years now: The Tim Tebow Problem. Tim Tebow was a quarterback for the Florida Gators from 2006-2009. He won the Heisman Trophy as the best player in college in 2008 and led his team to the National Championship in 2006 and 2008. So, in other words, he was one of the best quarterbacks in college football history. But, at the professional level, he did not achieve nearly the same level of success. He only lasted three years in the NFL with a well below average passer rating of 75 and completion percentage of 47. Why did Tebow struggle so much when he moved to the NFL?

Well, one of the main reasons that has been identified is his throwing mechanics[4]. In a nutshell, Tebow held the ball too low when dropping back to pass. This created two problems. First, it made him more likely to fumble when hit by a defender. Second, and more importantly, it substantially lengthened the time it takes to deliver the ball, giving defenders a better chance of sacking him before he throws. Tebow's throwing motion took roughly 0.6 sec to execute while the average for NFL quarterbacks is 0.4 sec. During his college career this 0.2 difference was not a big problem because most college defenders are a little bit slower. However, in the NFL with the world's best players, even a fraction of a second can make the difference. Referring back to Chapter 4, what happened here was a change in the *task constraints* facing Tebow. At the college level, defenders are going to be typically slower – creating lesser pressures on the coordination solution required to be a successful quarterback. When moving up to the NFL, it is possible that the solution used will no longer be effective.

So, why not just teach him to hold his hands higher? Well, I can tell you from many attempts to work on this technical issue with other quarterbacks - that is easier said than done! Along with the natural coordination tendencies we bring to the table when learning a new skill, it is also common for a performer to develop very deep attractors by practicing a skill a certain way for a long time. If our perceptual-motor landscape now has different hand position heights, Tebow dug himself a deep valley at the low position. All the interventions and instructions that coaches used when working with Tebow were fraught with the difficult problem of getting him to stay at an unstable region of his landscape and not fall into the deep, stable attractor valley.

I faced a similar problem when I started doing triathlons in my late 20's. I learned to swim in a lake where the only task constraints were making it to the raft without drowning. When the constraints of trying to swim faster and with better efficiency (so I had energy left for biking and running) were added in races, my Lake Simcoe swim stroke just did not quite cut it. And, like Tebow, I had a very difficult time trying to overcome the attractor and change my movement solution. In the parlance of movement science, Tim Tebow and I dug attractors that were *local minima* in the perceptual-motor landscape. Compared to nearby solutions they were effective but there were even better ones waiting to be found if we got out and explored a bit.

There are a couple critical points for coaching here. First, the athletes we work with are not blank slates. A movement solution is not created from nothing. It is built on top of the perceptual-motor landscape the athlete brings to the first day of practice. Every athlete has both their own intrinsic dynamics and, most likely, some attractors that have been created through early experience. Whether it is swimming in a lake, playing pick-up sports at recess, or playing catching with a parent, we start digging attractor valleys in our perceptual-motor landscape pretty much from the moment we start moving. This is yet another reason why the idea of the one, correct technique is a fallacy. Every, single athlete you coach is different. Every single one. Coaching is not building a house from ground up. It is a renovation and expansion. Success requires designing practice that builds on each performer's foundation.

A second key point we can learn from Tim Tebow and my swimming experience is that the movement solution we come up with, the attractor landscape we create, is shaped by the constraints we face when practicing a skill. Human beings are brutally efficient learners. If there is no pressure for a quarterback to get the ball out quickly, it is likely they will settle at a local minima with a slower delivery. If I do not have to run and bike when I am learning to swim it is not likely I am going to come up with a stroke that maximizes oxygen efficiency. As we will see in the coming chapters, effective coaching involves making sure that the constraints an athlete faces in practice encourage them to climb out of attractor valleys and explore the perceptual-motor landscape. And this is the answer to the question I posed earlier: what causes us to break free of the attractors in our perceptual-motor landscape? To learn to drum out more complex patterns, swim more efficiently, and hold the football higher? The answer is: changes in the constraints. So, let's see what happens when we do this…

Exploring the perceptual-motor landscape and the nonlinear nature of learning

In the second part of the Zanone and Kelso drumming study I mentioned earlier participants were asked to try and learn a relative phase that was not one of their intrinsic attractors. For example, a participant with strong attractors at 0 and 180 deg relative phase (like shown in the top panel of Figure 6.3) was asked to try and drum at 90 deg, while a participant with attractors at 0, 90 and 180 deg was asked to learn to play at 135 deg. How did the researchers encourage the learners to get out of their attractor valleys and move into these unstable regions? By adding a constraint. In this case it was informational one. Specifically, small little lights were presented which flashed at the desired drumming rhythm and participants were given feedback after each trial about any errors they were making.

Although all participants were successful in learning the new pattern, as shown in Figure 6.4, they did so in very different ways. The group learning the 90 degrees phase seemed to completely restructure their perceptual-motor landscape – they got out their shovels and dug a new attractor valley at 90 deg. This was accompanied with a large amount of variability as they explored different ways to produce this new rhythm. This type of learning, in which we switch to using a completely different coordination pattern that we never did before by creating a new attractor, is called *bifurcation*. The name reflects the fact that the performer is taking their perceptual-motor landscape and breaking it into new parts and regions of stability and instability.

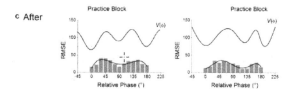

Figure 6.4 – Changes in the attractor landscape that occur through practice. From Kostrubiec et al. (2012).

For the group learning to drum at 135 deg the change was much less dramatic but equally as effective. As shown in the right panel of Figure 6.4, instead of digging a whole new attractor valley that wasn't there before, participants in this group seemed to just move their existing attractor from 90 to 135 deg. There was much less variability in their drumming performance suggesting that instead of doing wild exploration like the first group, their learning involved more of a gradual shift towards the desired pattern. This type of learning is referred to as a *shift*, reflecting the fact that we are not completely restructuring our perceptual-motor landscape and making new attractors but instead just shifting and re-organizing ones we already have. This difference again highlights the individual nature of learning a skill. In some cases, we will be able to work with what we got and make relatively small shifts or changes to our existing pattern of coordination. While, in others we will need to move to using a completely novel pattern with a bifurcation (or splitting apart) of our perceptual-motor landscape.

Results like these have also led to another important revolution in our understanding of how skill acquisition occurs. Think about how we have traditionally represented the changes in performance that occur as we practice something – the infamous *learning curve* shown in Figure 6.5. With practice we initially show very large improvements from day to day, then we hit the plateau where things get tough and many of us put that guitar back in the closet or stop showing up for those karate lessons. We are still making gains with practice, but they are much smaller and less motivating. Another feature of this traditional view is that the benefits we get from practice are fairly predictable. If we practice in the right way, focusing on achieving the correct technique, and put in the time we will get the continuous improvement we seek. This idea is captured in K. Ander's Ericsson's research on deliberate practice, famously popularized in the "10,000 rule" by Malcom Gladwell[5]. Ericsson's research showed that the level of skill achieved across a wide range of domains from chess to music to sports was mostly determined by the number of hours of deliberate practice (focused on differences between the learner's execution and an expert model) completed by the performer. So, in this traditional view, learning occurs in roughly a straight line that is determined and predictable from what we put into each session.

Figure 6.5 – The "learning curve".

While the learning curve is a nice story it is again a bit of a misleading fallacy. It suffers from the same problem I discussed in Chapter 1 – things getting lost in the average. The learning curve (including figures which relate the number of hours of deliberate practice to performance) is what we get when we combine data from several learners. As any coach will tell you, on an individual level, learning very rarely follows this nice smooth progression. We do not always see improvements in performance from session to session. Sometimes there are no gains, sometimes learners fall back to a lower level and in some practice sessions there is a sudden improvement that seems to come out of nowhere. This latter effect was exactly what we saw in the drumming study for participants that took the bifurcation route to learning. They went from stable performance with low errors but not at the desired phase to a large amount of variability with huge errors while they were exploring the perceptual motor landscape. Then, finally, the new desired pattern of 90 deg was found. There was not a continuous, incremental improvement in performance. Instead, the pattern of learning we get when we look at it the individual level is typically highly *nonlinear*.

This nonlinear pattern of learning is to be expected if we accept that we are all working at Self Organization LLC. Remember self-organization is a process that occurs when the lower levels of a system organize themselves in the presence of a set of constraints without any instructions from a boss. The net result is a *complex system* where the outputs we get are highly unpredictable - not smooth, continuous gains. To understand this point I want you to think about two very different endeavors one can pursue in life: sending a rocket to the moon or raising kids. Aerospace engineering is an example of a deterministic, complicated system. By that I mean the process is very difficult and complicated (it takes a lot of very smart people working together with a lot of knowledge) but the outcome is fairly predictable. For the most part, if the team follows all the correct steps in the process the outcome is highly reliable. We know what the output (successful moon landing) will be based on the inputs to the system.

Now consider raising children. If, like me, you have more than one you will have no doubt realized that the outputs (your child's development and behavior) are rarely predictable from the inputs (your parenting methods). Things that worked great for potty training or getting your first kid to sleep through the night are often completely ineffective when you try them on your other children. If you do not have children, think about the best party you have ever been to. What do you think would happen if you tried to perfectly recreate it? Invite the same people, serve the same food, play the same music, and hang out in the same part of the kitchen. Do you think it would be as good? Would the output be predictable from the input? I can tell you that I have actually tried this, and my single trail attempt was an abject failure! Raising children and parties are examples of non-deterministic, *complex* systems. In a complex system, the constraints (the individual child or party goer, environment created by the music or presence of other siblings, etc.) interact in highly unpredictable ways resulting in highly unpredictable and often frustratingly unexpected patterns of self-organization.

Embracing the complexity and individuality of skill acquisition

So, much like raising kids and throwing a great party, coaching is not rocket science. It is much, much harder! In this revolution in thinking about how we learn to perform new skills one of the first and most important steps is accepting and embracing this complexity. Learning is not a predictable process where we can just give an individual the "correct technique" and expect success. To best support skill acquisition, we need to change the conception of a coach from an instructor (I have the correct solution and I here to give it to you) to that of a *designer* and *guide*. An effective coach should attempt to design practice environments that foster exploration and promote self-organization rather that prescribing a solution to an athlete. In doing this, they need to take into account the foundation they are adding to (the intrinsic dynamics and attractors the performer already has) rather than ignoring their previous experiences and forcing the athlete to do things "my way". Coaches need to accept that in a complex system they cannot possibly know what the optimal movement solution for an individual athlete will be. They can only help them find it for themselves.

Critically, this also relates to the second part of effective coaching: being an informed and knowledgeable guide through the search process. The word "educate" comes from the word *educere*, which means "to lead out". We are helping someone on a path not giving them the answer. A common misconception about this new approach to skill is that it is just "set it and forget it". That is, once a coach designs practice, they must just let it run, without saying anything or stepping in. Just let them play games, don't coach them on how to do it. That could not be further from the truth. As we have seen in some of the examples discussed in the book already, like pitching in sand or changing equipment, in guiding an athlete a coach should use their experiential knowledge to identify movement solutions that will not be effective or will have the potential to produce injury. They should also be observing practice to see if athletes are not taking the opportunities for action (the affordances they are trying to amplify) they have created. In all these cases, the coach can and should step in and try to guide search in a different direction. In the next two chapters we will look at specific ways these coaching goals of designing effective practice activities and guiding search can be achieved.

7

NEW WAYS OF COACHING I: THE CONSTRAINTS-LED APPROACH (CLA)

L et's start with a problem. Like many sports skills baseball pitching requires the effective transfer of force. In order to throw the ball at high velocity the pitcher needs to take the ground reaction force they generate by pushing off the mound with their back foot and move it through their body to their hand holding the ball. In biomechanics we call this a *kinetic chain*. *Kinetic* referring to the fact we are talking about movement and *chain* to refer the fact that the different body parts involved in creating the movement connect to each other like the links in a chain. Movement of a pitcher's legs causes rotation of their hips, which moves their torso, shoulder, arm, and eventually their hand.

What happens when we break this chain? This is exactly what occurs in a common technical flaw that has been found in pitchers called *forearm flyout*[1]. As shown in Figure 7.1 (left panel), this involves the arm separating from the body too early in the pitching delivery, breaking the kinetic chain. This is problematic for two reasons. First, instead of the force moving through the large muscles in the pitcher's hips and torso it essentially jumps links in the chain and goes all into the small muscles of the arm which cannot create and transfer force nearly as effectively. The net result is they will likely throw at a velocity much lower than they could potentially generate if they kept the chain intact. And this leads to the second, more serious problem – a large amount force will be concentrated into the poor UCL ligament in the elbow we talked about back in Chapter 4. This dramatically increases the risk for injury and TJ surgery.

*Figure 7.1 – Fixing the problem of "forearm flyout"
in baseball pitching.*

So, if we are a pitching coach how do we go about getting the pitcher to change their delivery to something safer and more effective? The traditional way of coaching is, of course, to try to give them the "correct" pitching mechanics through some type of explicit instruction. For example, we could tell them to "bend your elbow 10 deg less at the top of your delivery" or "keep your arm against your body for half a second longer". I can tell you from personal experience that trying to give the pitcher the solution like this does not work very well at all. Let's try to pull together some pieces from previous chapters to understand why.

First, and foremost, trying to give the pitcher the "correct" mechanics does not fit at all with the business model of Self Organization LLC. We are trying to jump in and be the boss when the company does not have one! The angles, positions, and timing of the movements of the different body segments during a complex act like pitching are degrees of freedom that are going to be self-organized at the level of the muscles and joints - not given in a memo from the CEO's office. Consistent with this idea, research has shown that even highly skilled athletes are very poor at following detailed instructions about how to change or correct their technique.

Let's look at an example from tennis. In a 2015 study, Giblin and colleagues[2] asked eight internationally ranked tennis players to implement instructions like: "Increase your maximum knee flexion by 5%" or "move the point of racquet ball contact during your serve 10 cm forward". Motion tracking equipment was used to determine how effectively each player could do this. Two key findings emerged. First, although participants could successfully change their technique in some way, they had very large errors. For example, when asked to move their impact location 10 cm to the left, the mean absolute error was 15cm! In other words, this highly specific instruction "move 10cm left" resulted in impact points that were everything from 5cm to the right to 25 cm to left. The second finding was, that for most participants, the smaller changes (e.g., move 2.5 cm to the left) were less than the trail-to-trail variability in their movement. Remember in our "repetition without repetition" revolution we do not perform a skill the exact same way every time. Therefore, the amount of knee bend and impact location are going to be slightly different on every execution. In this tennis study, the average trial to trial variability was roughly 3.5% (with a maximum of 7%) for knee flexion and 10 cm (with a maximum of 14cm) for the impact location. It is not surprising that the tennis players could not implement the instructions about the ONE way we want them to serve because they don't serve in just one way to begin with! How can I possibly be expected to implement a 2.5% change in angle or a 5cm change in position when these aspects of my movement are varying by more than that already?

The second major problem with trying to correct technical flaws like forearm flyout by giving the athlete the solution through explicit instruction is that, even when you can get the athlete to implement the change, it tends not to be very "sticky". That is, after practice is over and the athlete goes back into competition, it is common for them to revert back to their old technique. This seems to particularly the case when the athlete gets in a high-pressure situation. For example, in a study some colleagues and I published a few years ago we looked at the effects of pressure on golf putting performance[3]. In the putting studies I have done over the years a key difference in technique that seems to separate highly skilled and novice golfers is how they change their stroke to putt from longer distances. Or stated another way: how they adapt to a change in task constraints! Whereas lesser skilled golfers tend to putt further by increasing the speed of the stroke, experts increase the length of their stroke. The problem with the movement solution used by novices is described nicely by instructor Dave Pelz:

"We tested the putting stoke of some 150 amateurs at the DuPont World Amateur Tournament. The averaged results show that the length of their backswings varied only about 6 inches, while the length of the putts produced varied 6 to 30 feet. This means the backswing, the power generator of the putting stroke, varied only 6 inches for 24 feet...Think of the pressure that putts on every putt. These amateurs must be able to sense and feel a difference of less than one inch to produce putts of 12 and 15 feet, respectively."[4]

But interestingly the solution used changed for some of the golfers when we offered money for making putts and put scores up on a big leaderboard for the other participants to see. Specifically, some of the experienced golfers in our study holed significantly fewer putts in the pressure condition that they did in a non-pressure pre-test – what we would commonly call "choking". For these golfers, there was also a significant reduction in the relationship between the length of the putting stroke and the distance to the hole. At the other extreme, some of the golfers in our study were "clutch", holing significantly more puts under pressure and taking all our money. For these golfers, there was no change in their putting technique when pressure was added. Linking this back to the topic of embodied perception we looked at in Chapter 5, in a separate study we showed that golfers that "choke" and change their movement solution under pressure also perceive the hole to shrink in size.

What might cause a performer to change their movement solution to a less effective one under pressure? As first purposed by Rich Masters it could have something to with the way they were taught their skill in the first place. Master's Reinvestment Theory[5] argues that when we learn via a coach's detailed, explicit instructions about the "correct" technique, it is possible that we will revert back to these instructions (like a child grabbing their safety blanket) when under pressure. So, in other words, a skilled golfer might start thinking about "keeping their head down" and "their feet shoulder width apart" when they have a putt to win a tournament. Evidence for this idea can be seen in a recent study by Lola & Tzetzis[6]. In the key comparison, a group that was given explicit instructions about how to serve a volleyball (e.g., "the left hand holds the volleyball extended forward in front of your right side") was compared to a group that received no instructions and instead just practiced on their own after watching demonstration videos. While there was no significant difference between the groups at the end of training, when pressure was added (having to be observed by scouts) the serving accuracy of the group trained with explicit instructions dropped by nearly 20% while the no-instruction maintained their accuracy at the same level. So, not only is it difficult for a performer to take on board explicit instructions about movement technique, even when they "work" they do not seem to be very pressure proof! There has to be a better way..

An alternative: Promoting exploration through constraints manipulation

Returning to our pitcher with forearm flyout, if we can't just give them the solution to fix this issue, what can we do instead? Believe it or not the answer to the question for me and many other coaches came from looking in a kids toybox. As shown in Figure 7.1 (and can be seen in the video here[7]) a common coaching method now used to address this problem is practicing with a connection ball. With this, the pitcher is given a new goal for the practice activity: move so that, when you pitch, the connection ball goes towards the plate when it flies out. No other instruction about how to achieve this or feedback is given. Although this may seem quite simple, it perfectly illustrates the four key principles of an increasingly popular method of coaching called the constraints-led approach or CLA. In the CLA, one or more constraints are manipulated in practice in order to:

1) De-stabilize the existing movement solution/attractor

As we saw in Chapter 6, one of the real challenges faced by a coach is trying to overcome the existing attractors and coordination tendencies of a performer. And this is definitely true with my pitching example. Most of the pitchers I have worked with that exhibit forearm flyout have been pitching that way (usually very successfully) for years. Just like Tim Tebow in college, the flyout solution was highly effective in the face of the constraints they had faced up to this point. So, there tends to be a very deep attractor valley around the elbow angle being used. How do we get them out of it and make them explore other solutions without getting pulled back in?

This is why we call it a constraint! We are taking away something, constraining you from using a particular solution. The first reason we add the task constraint of the connection ball is that makes the pitcher's existing movement solution ineffective for achieving the new goal we have given them. If you separate your arm from your body early in the delivery, the ball will fall out and go to the side, every time. In this new, strange world where we are making you pitch with a big, yellow rubber ball under your arm, the pitcher's existing solution no longer offers stability. This is incentive to explore..

2) Encourage exploration and self-organization

Notice that at no point did we tell the pitcher about how to make the connection ball go forwards towards the plate. We gave no instructions about how to position their elbow or when to move their arm. Instead of pushing them towards the one, correct solution, our goal here is to get them to explore the perceptual-motor landscape, and allow for self-organization of a new solution that works for them. In using the CLA, we recognize that we do not know the solution to the problem of forearm flyout that will work for this individual we are coaching and even if we did there is no effective way to just give it to them through explicit instruction.

3) Amplify information and invite affordances

As we saw in Chapter 5, our perceptual-motor system is not re-creating that world in our head but is instead picking up information and action opportunities that can be used to achieve our specific goal at hand. But it is often the case that lesser-skilled performers, are not yet tuned into these information sources. A particularly common example of this I see when working with young athletes is a lack of sensitivity to information about body position and body movement – termed our internal senses of *proprioception* and *kinesthesis.* Try standing on one foot with your other leg bent so your heel is against the side of your straight, supporting leg (what is known as the tree pose in yoga). Now close your eyes. Did you fall over? Hopefully not, but for most the task of maintaining balance becomes more difficult. When we take away vision we must rely on our internal senses (signals coming from our joints, muscles and tendons) to maintain balance and most of us are just not that sensitive to this information. One of the main reasons why is that we do not have a lot of practice using it. We spend most of the time acting with our eyes open and we are very visually dominant creatures.

. . .

In the CLA , another goal is to give the athlete more opportunities to use information sources and experience affordances than they would not get from just playing their sport. Examples of this include giving athletes more opportunities to perceive and act on gaps between players in sports like basketball and soccer by reducing the size of the field (a practice activity known as *small-sided games* we will look at in detail shorty) and giving athlete more opportunity to use their internal senses by blocking or restricting vision in some way in practice (which we will see in Chapter 13 when looking at some new training technologies). Returning to the connection ball, the athlete is being provided with information about the relative timing of the movement of the arm and the rest of the body (through the pressure of the connection ball against their skin) that they do not get during normal pitching. In the CLA, we are amplifying information that typically has a low volume so that the performer can hopefully incorporate into their new movement solution.

4) Provide Transition Feedback about the Effectiveness of the Search

If we are going to encourage an athlete to get out there and explore, how do we know we are guiding them to a bountiful garden full of food and not off the edge of a cliff? The very challenging question of how to know whether the search for a movement solution is effective is something I will tackle in detail in Chapter 9. But, if possible, one way that a coach can help an athlete explore effectively is by adding a constraint that creates what Karl Newell has termed *transition feedback*[8]. In movement science, we typically talk about two kinds of feedback: knowledge of results (KR) and knowledge of performance (KP). KR feedback provides information about how close the outcome of your action was to your goal. So, in our connection ball practice activity, this would be whether or not you hit the catcher's target when pitching the baseball (which is still your primary goal). KP feedback provides information about the process underlying the result. So, in baseball pitching, we could provide feedback about the pitcher's arm velocity or elbow angle. This results/performance division is something we now see in many walks of life. For example, in my job it's how many grants you were awarded vs how many proposals you submitted.

Transition feedback is something quite different. Instead of telling you about whether you achieved your goal or about the underlying processes, it tells you whether your search for a better solution is headed in the correct direction. When I first try the connection ball with a pitcher, the connection ball will almost go directly to the side when it falls out. But, as shown nicely in the video linked above, with a bit of practice it starts going a bit more forwards. In this activity, the direction the ball goes when it falls out provides transition feedback. If it starts going more forwards, whatever you changed about your delivery is taking you towards a more effective solution. If it starts going more to the side, you need to explore elsewhere.

Another way to think about what the CLA is trying to achieve is that it is adding *structured variability* to practice. In traditional coaching, we are trying to reduce variability as much as possible by getting the athlete to repeat the exact same movement. With the CLA we are accepting that movement variability and exploration of different solutions is functional. Of course, it is also important to note that we are following the basic business principles of Self Organization LLC here – using context dependent, whole (not modularized training). Let's look at another commonly used example of the CLA in action…

Small-sided and conditioned games

Soccer is a game that relies critically on interpersonal interactions. Driving the ball pass a defender on the dribble, threading a pass between two defenders, or perfectly playing a long ball on to the foot of your teammate that is making a run. But think about the layout of a soccer pitch. Excluding the goalkeepers, there are 22 players on a field with typical dimensions of 136 x 93 yards. That's 575 square yards or about 1725 square feet per player. I have lived in houses where I am closer to my neighbor! Practicing on a regulation soccer field with the regulation number of players provides us with relatively few opportunities to interact directly, in close proximity to opponents and teammates. Or, put another way, the volume of the information used to control actions like passing and doing a dribble drive is not very loud. Players get very few opportunities to learn how their actions influence the interpersonal distance between themselves, opponents and teammates.

One way that this is being addressed by many coaches now, in soccer as well as other team sports that have similar issues like basketball, ice hockey and field hockey, is by using another type of CLA manipulation: the small-sided game. In a small-sided game, the task constraints facing the players are changed by reducing the number of players and/or the size of the playing area. So, for example, in soccer we might setup a practice activity with four players per team and using a 30 x 30 yard area of the pitch – reducing the area per player to 112 square yards or 338 square feet. Let's look at what this achieves in terms of our four goals of the CLA.

First, using a small-sided game is going to de-stabilize movement solutions in which players are avoiding getting into the fray and acting in close quarters with other players. Due to the dramatic reduction in square footage, it is more difficult for players to hold or dribble the ball, so they are keeping away from opponents. Instead, they must get used to moving into smaller spaces, making quick decisions when an opponent is closing in on them, finding ways to get around an opponent instead of always moving into open space etc. You can no longer hide in the corner of your big 1700 square foot apartment! This is particularly important in sports that allow for physical contact like ice hockey.

Second, if it is done correctly, small-sided games encourage self-organization and exploration for new movement solutions. When the number of players and field dimensions are changed, the plays that a coach has drawn up on the whiteboard for their team to run are typically no longer going to work. Instead, the players must work together to come up with new ways to move the ball and create scoring opportunities. Players are going to find themselves in different positions relative to the goal and defenders than they are used to. This can be further exacerbated if a coach uses unbalanced numbers in their practice activity (e.g., 4x3, 5x3).

Third, small-sided games amplify information and present new affordances to players. They give a player more opportunities to experience the coupling between their actions and information sources like interpersonal distance and relative velocity of other players. This is likely to help them become more sensitive to these perceptual information sources and encourage them to explore ways to achieve key performance outcomes – for example, maintain or breakdown the stability of the interpersonal distance. This is difficult to achieve during full sided games on a regulation sized field because the systems are much more stable, groups of players are often inactive and uninvolved and, therefore it is harder for an individual player to destabilize the system. Small-sided games also give players more opportunities to experiences sub-phases of play that can occur in a game, for example a 3 on 1 break, and learn how they can most effectively stabilize or destabilize such a situation. They help players to learn the action capabilities of their teammates (e.g., the different speeds at which players run into open space) which is critical for developing teamwork. Finally, as we will examine in detail in Chapter 11, the use of small-sided games can also increase the amount of time spent in playful and enjoyable activities by allowing learners to experience simulations of competitive team games, as opposed to running boring old drills.

Small-sided games can also increase the transition feedback players receive to help guide their exploration. When I drive forward with the ball in soccer or reverse the direction of flow with a crosscourt pass in basketball in a small-sided game, I will get immediate feedback about how this influences the positions and movement of the other players. This information can be used to guide my exploration for new movement solutions.

All the effects I have just described can also be further enhanced by using *conditioned games* in conjunction with a small-sided game.

In a conditioned game, the task constraints are manipulated by changing the rules. For example, if a coach wanted to emphasize ball movement, they could add a rule to the practice activity that players cannot shoot until they have made at least five passes. If a coach wanted to emphasize fore-checking in hockey, they could add a rule that a goal scored after a turnover is worth 2 points instead of 1. Again, we are changing the constraints to push the performer into a different area of the perceptual-motor landscape.

One final point here. The use of small-sided games is often cited as evidence that the CLA approach to coaching is "old wine in new bottles". That is, it is nothing new, we are just using fancier words like de-stabilize, constraints and affordances to describe it. While it is true that coaches have been reducing the number of players and size of the playing area for a long time, it was typically not done with goals that were compatible with the CLA. For example, a common experience that I have had in observing soccer and hockey practices over the years is for coaches to set up as small sided or conditioned game, let the players start, then stop it in less than a minute so that they correct something that was done wrong (e.g., a player not passing to the correct teammate). Clearly, this is not promoting self-organization and exploration but rather using smaller numbers and smaller spaces to coach ideal solutions.

The Use of Analogies

As a final example of the CLA let's look at how informational constraints can be manipulated. A common misconception about the CLA is that it is "silent coaching". That is, once you design the practice activity (whether it is using a connection ball or a small-sided game) you must just stand back and let players figure it out on their own (self-organization is the key remember) without saying anything. This is simply not true. A verbal instruction to a player is a type of task constraint (in this case, an informational one) that can and should be used. Instead of precluding the use of explicit instructions to performers about how to move, in the CLA we use instructions in a different way and with different frequency. A good example of this of using analogies in coaching.

In a study published in 2014, Lee and colleagues compared two different ways of coaching 10-year-olds to execute a forehand stroke in tennis[9]. One of the key differences between the groups was the verbal instructions they were given. The traditionally coached group were given instructions that prescribed the one correct technique. One of the instructions was one commonly given to novice tennis players: "move the racquet low to high, by turning the shoulders to the side and contacting the ball in front of forward foot". The CLA group was told: "hit the ball like the shape of a rainbow". Let's compare and contrast these instructions.

First, note they are essentially both trying to achieve the same thing: encourage the player to use a movement solution which has a certain form. Remember, as we saw in Chapter 6, working at Self Organization LLC is not to deny that skillful movement has *invariant* properties. That is, there are some features common to the movement solutions used by elite athletes within a given sport that we want to try to encourage our athletes to use. In the CLA we are using *structured variability* – we want to allow the performer to explore and try different things, but we are pushing them to certain areas within the perceptual-motor landscape that we have identified as being key for an effective movement solution, whether it is keeping the kinetic chain intact when pitching or using a low to high stroke trajectory in tennis.

But look at the very different ways this invariance is being achieved with the two instructions. In traditional coaching, we get your movement to have the key invariant features by telling you how to produce them. We make specific reference to your body movements and positions - "turn your shoulders", "..in front of your forward foot". In other words, we are trying to give you the solution to the problem so that you can learn to reproduce it. In this CLA example, we are trying to encourage your movement solution to have a certain form by appealing to an analogy – a metaphor for the pattern of movement that does not refer to its specifics. When I tell you to move "like a rainbow", the key feature that comes to mind for most people is an arch in the path. Other examples of analogies that have been used in coaching are "move as if you are trying to put a cookie in a jar that is on a high shelf" for basketball free throws and "grip the club like you are holding a tube of toothpaste so that you don't squeeze any out" for golf putting. Instead of trying to give you the exact solution to the problem we are using an analogy to convey its key features. This has several advantages over the traditional approach. It does not require performers to implement highly specific technical changes (which we saw earlier in this chapter, we are not very good at), it avoids specific references to the performer's body which can lead to reinvestment and choking under pressure, and most critically, it allows for variability and individuality. We are encouraging athletes to produce the key properties of the movement form (the invariants), but we are giving them to freedom to use different movement solutions to produce it.

And this was exactly what was found in the study by Lee and colleagues. Using a technique called principal components analysis, the authors were able to group participants into clusters based on their movements. For example, some participants used more shoulder motion while others used more wrist. Before the training, both groups showed four clusters, or, other words, they used four different types of movement solutions. After training, the group that were given traditional prescriptive instructions not surprisingly became more homogenous – they now exhibited only three different clusters of solutions, As expected, the CLA group showed the opposite result – after training they exhibited eight clusters. This is an example of the biological degeneracy we saw back in Chapter 2 – the same function (an effective forehand) is being achieved by combining different body parts in different ways. A little more shoulder rotation here, a little more wrist action there. Why is this beneficial? Well, if as Nadal claims *"every shot is different; every single one."*, it would seem likely that we need a lot more than just THE ONE forehand stroke.

The key features of the CLA are summarized in the infographic shown in Figure 7.2 and we will see more examples in future chapters. But let's next turn to a different way of promoting self-organization and adaptability through practice design...

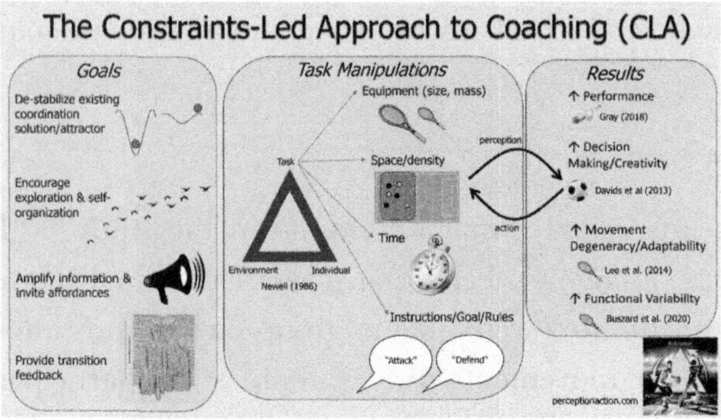

Figure 7.2 – Constraints-Led Approach (CLA) to Coaching Infographic

8

NEW WAYS OF COACHING II:
DIFFERENTIAL LEARNING

A nd now for something completely different! So, you want
to learn the how to start effectively in a speed skating race?
In your next five practice attempts I want you to do the following:
"Put your right hand on the ice and point your left arm forward",
"take very big steps", "take very small steps", "skate with your
arms held straight up in the air", "perform a pirouette before you
start". Or maybe you want to learn how to receive a pass with
your chest in soccer? For your next four practice attempts I want
you to do the following: "keep your right eye closed and hold
your left arm up in the air", "keep your feet close together, your
arms next to your body", "stand on your tippy toes and rotate
both arms in a windmill", "control the ball with your chest,
except it's going to be a beach ball". Believe it or not all of these
are actual instructions that were given to athletes in published
studies using the method of differential learning[1]. If you want to
see for yourself, go here and check it out (https://
perceptionaction.com/dl/). To quote the inventor of this
technique, Wolfgang Schollhorn: "If we want to have

III

extraordinary performance we need to train extraordinarily"
Mission accomplished!

What is going on here? How do these practice activities that seem
very odd on the surface and nothing like what an athlete might
do in competition help to improve performance? Differential
learning shares some similarities with the CLA. It has goals of
de-stabilizing the performer's existing movement
solutions/attractors, promoting exploration of the perceptual-
motor landscape, self-organization, and creating variability in
movement execution. However, it achieves these things in very
different ways. To understand this fascinating method, let's start
at the beginning.

When we show up at practice, we all bring our own level of
inherent variability. While, as we have seen, no performer moves in
exactly the same way on each execution of a skill, some of us are
more consistent than others. In the tennis study by Giblin and
colleagues we looked at last chapter, some of the players had
relatively small differences in their knee angle from serve to serve
(with standard deviations less than 2 deg) while others were much
less consistent (with standard deviations of angle greater than 5
deg). Similarly, in terms of racquet-ball contact point, some
players executed each serve within a relatively small space
(standard deviation of 7-8 cm) while others use contacts points
spread over almost twice that area. These differences can be
attributed to differences in the intrinsic dynamics we saw in
Chapter 6: each of our perceptual-motor landscapes have
different layouts, with deeper and shallower attractors. As we will
dive into detail in Chapter 9, some of this variability is good as it

reflects adaptation to changing constraints. For example, when the performer tosses the ball slightly more forward than usual, they will likely need to bend their knees slightly differently to hit it. But some of it is likely also bad variability as it involves movement patterns that are making performance unsuccessful. In differential learning we are trying to enhance the good while reducing the bad.

Think of these fluctuations in knee angles and ball contact positions like the random dots in the images we saw back in Figure 2.1. On the surface, they seem to be just noise that makes it harder to see the image. But just as we saw in that figure, the addition of more noise (more dots) on top of what is already there can actually makes things better. In differential learning, the primary goal of practice is to add fluctuations in movement on top of the performer's inherent variability with the intent of increasing the strength of the signal (the movement solution). Through the process of stochastic resonance we saw in Chapter 2, we pull out the signal from the noise by adding more noise[2]. This is achieved in practice by adding random fluctuations to the training environment in the form of very different body positions (feet together or apart, arms up or down), body movements (arms rotating in circles, legs moving slow or fast), perceptual information (one eye closed or both open) and/or equipment (beach balls vs soccer balls). Before we look at more specific examples and the results they produce, let's consider some of the key characteristics of this method.

1) Adding random variability to the practice environment to promote stochastic resonance

To illustrate the difference between the CLA and differential learning, I like to use the analogy of a food buffet. Imagine you are a doctor, and a patient has come to you that needs to change their diet. Our goal is in many ways like what a coach faces when using one of these methods. We want to get the person to move away from their current eating habits (those cheeseburgers they gravitate to every time at the buffet) and get them to explore other things, hopefully finding other, healthier foods they like. If we were using a CLA approach to this problem we might give them a constraint: you can only eat from the left side of the buffet with the salad bar. We are structuring their exploration by having them head to a particular area in the solution space we want them to be. A differential learning approach to the same problem would be something like: try the salad bar today, the seafood tomorrow, and the deli section the next day. Whereas the CLA seeks to structure the variability in practice and search, differential learning involves adding random, stochastic variability.

Using a differential learning approach does not involve trying to identify key task constraints and guide learning by manipulating them, instead it attempts to de-stabilize the existing movement solution by amplifying the natural fluctuations in the system (the inherent variability in athlete) through the addition of stochastic (random) perturbations in the practice environment. This allows the athlete to take full advantage of their own individual characteristics.

2) Perturbing the system, NOT getting the athlete to move in practice like they will move in the game

With most CLA manipulations, the goal is to guide an athlete to a movement solution (or a set of solutions) that will be transferable to competition. We want the baseball pitcher using the connection ball keep their arm closer to the body, soccer players participating in small-sided games to utilize space to create opportunities and de-stabilize an opponent's defense, and a tennis player to keeping swing "like a rainbow" during their next match in their next competition just like they are doing in practice. Obviously, as can be seen from the examples given at the start of the chapter, this is not the case for differential learning. We do not want to a speed skater to start with both hands in the air or do a pirouette at the next Olympics! Most of the variations the athlete experiences using differential learning in practice will likely never be used in competition. They are designed to randomly perturb the system and...

3) Allow the performer to gain information about solution space that can be used in future performances

As we saw back in Chapter 4, a solution space represents all possible combinations of degrees of freedom we could potentially use in our movement solution. In most cases, athletes only get to experience a very small area within this space because there are pushed towards a certain area of it in traditional, prescriptive coaching ("keep your elbow bent at 45 deg", etc..). In the CLA, our goal is to try and get you to move to a different area within this solution space that we have identified as being a more effective solution (e.g., keeping your arm closer to the body to prevent breaking the kinetic chain). Conversely, in differential learning, we want the athlete to explore all corners of it and learn to be able to interpolate between the executed movements. We are using perturbations in the practice conditions as information so the athlete can learn from them. If we assume that no movement will be repeated twice (a la Bernstein) then the more an athlete has explored the solution space, the more they will be able to adapt to the inevitable change in constraints. For example, maybe one of shots Nadal has never faced before (remember, they are all different) will require an off-balance backhand between the legs. In differential learning, it is hoped that by making the athlete practice using unusual postures and motions, they will be able to come up with unusual, extraordinary solutions like this in competition.

4) Creating the optimal level of noise for the individual athlete

As we will see in more detail in Chapter 11 when looking at youth sports coaching, a key to effectively using any coaching method that promotes variability in practice is ensuring that the amount added is appropriate for the individual athlete you are working with. We want the amount we add to be inversely related to the amount of inherent variability the athlete brings to practice themselves. So, for example, for the tennis players that has a large standard deviation in knee bend we want to have less variation in things like serve direction (e.g., we may want them to practice all crosscourt serves within a session) and effort (e.g., we may always want them to serve at 80% effort). While for players with the smaller standard deviation in knee bend we may want to vary these things, mixing in crosscourt and down the line serves and levels of effort (50,%, 80%, maximum). The reason we do this can be understood by again referring back to Figure 2.1. While the optimal amount of noise can enhance the signal, too much can start to degrade it again. When an athlete brings their own fluctuations to the field or court we need to add less as a coach to achieve the stochastic resonance we are looking for.

Consistent with this idea, research has shown the benefits of adding random conditions to practice are significantly lower in situations with more natural variability: field studies instead of experiments done in a lab, and younger, less-experienced athletes instead of adults.

Along with the athlete's inherent variability, there are other important factors that determine how big the fluctuations we add to practice should be when using differential learning. These include, how far is the solution you are asking them to perform from their existing solution (e.g., are you asking an athlete that normally uses a narrow stance to adopt a wide one), age (in general younger athletes will require less variability in practice), and skill level (in general, novices need less). Another factor is the nature of the change in movement solution you are asking the athlete to make (or mathematical order, for the math-inclined). In general, positional perturbations (i.e., 0 order, "keep your arm straight") will be less of a perturbation than velocity perturbations (1, "move your right arm faster than your left") which are less than acceleration perturbations (2) which are less than rhythm perturbations i.e., "jerk" (3).

Finally, an important factor that is often overlooked when using challenging coaching methods like differential learning (and the CLA) is that their success will depend heavily on how effectively an athlete responds to being challenged and how willing they are to make mistakes in practice. Do they get easily frustrated when they fail? Like many athletes, do they feel like they are always be scouted and evaluated such that they need to be as close to perfect as possible on every execution? If so, they are not going to respond very well to large perturbations we might add because they are likely to make them fail. So, we might want to start by adding a bit less variability to practice.

Comparative research on Self-Organization & Traditional Coaching Methods

A comment I often get when talking about new coaching methods like the CLA and differential learning is: show me the proof! Provide evidence that these approaches work better than traditional methods designed to give an athlete the "correct" solution. Well, here you go! Table 8.1 shows all the studies that I am aware of at the time of writing that have made direct comparisons between methods. As any new ones have come out since you can find an updated table here: https://perceptionaction.com/comparative/

Study	Coaching Method	Sport	Findings
Beckham & Schollhorn (2003)	Differential Learning (DL)	Shot put	Greater distance in DL group
Savlesbergh et al (2010)	DL	Speed Skating	Faster times for DL group
Schollhorn et al (2012)	DL	Soccer	Greater shooting and passing accuracy for DL groups
Lee et al (2014)	CLA (Constraints Led Approach)	Tennis	No significant performance differences but larger variety of solutions (degeneracy) for CLA group
Hossner et al (2016), Experiment 1	DL	Soccer	No significant differences
Hossner et al (2016), Experiment 2	DL	Shot Put	No significant differences
Gray (2018)	CLA	Baseball	Greater launch angle, exit velocity and more home runs for CLA group
Gray (2020)	DL, CLA	Baseball	More hits for the CLA group
Orangi et al (2021)	DL, CLA	Soccer	Both CLA and DL lowered risk factors for ACL injury

Table 8.1 – Results from studies directly comparing traditional prescriptive coaching with either the CLA, Differential Learning or both. For a more up-to-date version please see: https://perceptionaction.com/comparative/

Overall, there is pretty strong evidence in support of the coaching methods aimed at promoting self-organization. Three studies (examining shot putt, speed skating, soccer) have found significant performance benefits to differential learning training. Specifically, athletes threw further, skated faster and passed more accurately after differential learning training as compared to the same amount of time training with traditional methods which attempt to prescribe an ideal solution. And, as I will discuss in more detail in Chapter 13, I have found these methods work better in coaching baseball batting in two separate studies.

Developing Adaptable vs Adjustable Athletes

To end this discussion, I want to highlight one more key difference between these self-organization focused methods and traditional coaching: the purpose of adding variability to practice. To be clear, as I mentioned when looking at small-sided games, adding variations to the practice conditions like the size of the field, what type of serve they perform, or the body posture they adopt is not new and is not something exclusive to the CLA and differential learning. In fact, the effects of adding variability to practice has been one of the most well studied topics in movement science. Beginning with work of Richard Schmidt in the 1970's, it has long been known that varying up the practice conditions (instead of keeping everything the same) results in superior skill acquisition. The most well studied example of this the difference between blocked (where we perform the same skill over and over) and random practice (where we mix in different skills). For more information on this body of research, please see the resource page I have created: https://perceptionaction.com/vp/

. . .

However, even though variability of practice conditions has been used in traditional coaching, it gives very different answers when we ask "why", "when" and "how". A good way to think about this issue is how the two different approaches relate practice variability, movement variability and outcome variability. As shown in Figure 8.2 for baseball batting, in the traditional approach, it is assumed that low outcome variability (consistently hitting the ball in the middle of the barrel of the bat – which we want no matter what approach we take to coaching), is achieved through low movement variability (having a repeatable swing). So, repetition (of outcome) through repetition (of movement). To achieve this, we typically start with low variability in practice conditions (e.g., hitting of a tee) because we want the performer to learn the "correct" technique first before they plug it into more variable game conditions. Therefore, the purpose of adding variability is to allow the performer to develop *adjustability* of the ideal technique to specific variations in environmental conditions that will occur in competition. For example, to keep the ideal swing for both fast and slow pitches, to have a "correct" golf swing both on flat ground or a downhill slope, or to execute an accurate soccer pass from short and long distances. This is the "why".

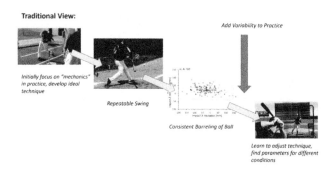

Figure 8.2. The relationship between practice, movement and outcome variability in the traditional approach to skill acquisition

As far as the "when" goes, if we follow this approach, we want to add higher variability relatively late in the skill acquisition process because we need the basic technique already developed first. That is why we start training with athletes dribbling around cones, hitting off tees, and always practicing golf swings on flat ground. We are purposely reducing the variability and removing things like decision making because the "correct" technique is best established through low variability, repeatable conditions. There is a lot of research evidence consistent with this idea. For example, we know that a basic level of performance (under the same conditions) is acquired faster in blocked as compared to random conditions – it is only later in retention and transfer tests that random becomes superior. Another example is the Lee et al tennis study we looked in Chapter 6. In that study, the group that had lower variability in practice not surprisingly scored higher on ratings of technical proficiency made by a coach after training as compared to a high variability training group. If you want a performer to develop one ideal technique, low variability is the way to start.

. . .

Now, what about the "how"? Remember the goal of adding variability here is to get the performer to elaborate on their existing movement solution so it can be maintained and be effective under different conditions that might occur in real competition. This means we should ideally be doing two things in terms of how variability is used. First, the things we vary in practice (speed, distance, spacing of players) should be things that will vary in the game. It makes no sense at all to add something that would never occur (e.g., a larger than normal ball or closing one eye). Why would we want our solution to be able to adjust to such things if they are going to never happen in a game? Second, the coach should give corrective feedback about any deviations in technique that occur in response to the new variations in conditions. This could come in the form of cues to get the performer back to the ideal movement they developed under low variability conditions ("remember you need to keep your knees bent") or in the form of an instruction that tells the performer specifically how the movement solution needs to be adjusted to a specific variation (e.g. "when hitting on a downhill position the ball back in your stance.."). So, in nutshell, in this approach the goal is: *repetition with repetition despite variation.*

Now, let's contrast this with the self-organization approaches like the CLA and differential learning. Referring again to the relationship between the different types of variability, as shown in Figure 8.2 in this approach it is proposed that low outcome variability REQUIRES a significant degree of movement variability (because the internal and external conditions are dynamic and changing). So, repetition (of outcome) without repetition (of movement). To achieve this, we want to introduce variability right at the beginning of training to encourage exploration of the perceptual-motor landscape and learning to solve movement problems. Successful performance in the real, dynamic sporting environment requires the use of different (not one ideal) movement solutions because the constraints are ever-changing. The purpose of practice variability here is to develop *adaptability* in being able to solve movement problems not to develop adjustability of an already developed technique. That is the "why".

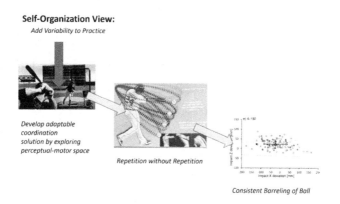

Self-Organization View:
Add Variability to Practice

Develop adaptable coordination solution by exploring perceptual-motor space

Repetition without Repetition

Consistent Barreling of Ball

Figure 8.2. The relationship between practice, movement and outcome variability in the self-organization approach to skill acquisition

In terms of "when", we want a relatively high degree of variability from the start. So instead of tees, cones, and flat ground we want thrown balls, interactions with opponents and changing ground conditions.

Finally, "how" variability is implemented is also very different than in the traditional approach. Variations in the practice conditions that would never occur in actual competition are not only OK, but they are also desirable! Remember we are trying to teach the performer to problem solve (i.e., self-organize into a coordination solution that meets the goal in face of the constraints they face) and to "learn to learn to move". We are not trying to teach them to come up with specific adjustments of solutions to specific variations of conditions they might face in the game. Using different sized balls, weird body postures and closing one or the other eye as is used in differential learning, are all good here because they all require the performer to solve a movement problem.

The key components of the Differential Learning method of coaching are illustrated in the infographic shown in Figure 8.3. Let's next consider in detail whether or not all this variability and exploration is leading us astray.

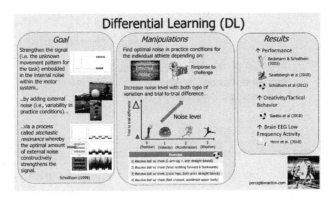

Figure 8.3 – Differential Learning infographic

9

GOOD VS BAD VARIABILITY, OPTIMAL MOVEMENT SOLUTIONS & EFFECTIVE SELF-ORGANIZATION

I don't know about you, but I don't remember using connection balls in baseball practice or doing pirouettes during power skating practice as a kid. Coaching methods like the CLA and differential learning are clearly radically different than the traditional way most of us have been taught movement skills. Instead of trying to get us to consistently repeat one ideal movement solution given by a coach or instructor, they are encouraging exploration, variability in movement and self-organization. But with this new view there are some key questions that arise that I often get asked by coaches. Surely, not all kinds of movement variability are beneficial? Surely, there are times when the performer is going to explore their way into a self-organized movement solution that is just not much better (and maybe even worse) than the one I pushed them away from? If, as coaches, we are guides and designers not instructors, how do we know we are not leading people astray?

What is a "good" self-organized movement solution?

In order to understand what types of movement solutions a performer might self-organize into and address the question of whether these are good, we need to first consider the stage of skill acquisition the performer is at. Are they a complete novice to the skill or have them been practicing it for a while? This is something that Bernstein thought a lot about. He proposed that the movement solutions adopted by performer's first learning a skill would go through three distinct stages.

Freezing and Freeing Degrees of Freedom

As we saw in Chapter 4, one of the first solutions that many learners use when practicing a new skill is freezing degrees of freedom. That is, they take some body parts out of the equation by not moving them at all or couple two different body parts so that they move together. Are these freezing solutions good? Well, maybe it is better to say they are good enough. Freezing is a simple and easy way to solve the degrees of freedom and gain some initial proficiency in the task which allows the athlete to start playing the game. Imagine, if instead of using a simple underhand serve in volleyball, we forced you to learn a full jump serve (involving multiple degrees of freedom in the lower and upper body) before getting into a match. It is very likely that you would get frustrated, lose interest in the sport, and move onto something else. As discussed in Chapter 11, we do this in a lot of sports by making kids play with adult equipment like full size basketball hoops and tennis racquets.

But there are also some major limitations to freezing as a movement solution. First, it does not allow the performer to take full advantage of external forces in the environment. Think back to the kinetic chain we talked about in Chapter 7. Freezing degrees of freedom is essential removing links. Instead of transferring force by pushing off from the ground, the tennis player in Figure 4.4 is generating all the force just from shoulder rotation. This is going to result in a serve that has much lower velocity than could be achieved if we incorporated other degrees of freedom. Second, freezing solutions are not very adaptable. In volleyball, just rotation around your shoulder or coupling your shoulder and elbow movement is not going to give you many options from placing the ball and taking advantage of the other team's defensive alignment. Furthermore, these solutions are not going to be very resilient to your own inherent variability. For example, if the server holds the ball slightly higher or releases it slightly earlier with the lead hand (like the variation we saw in the tennis serve data in Chapter 7), it will be difficult for them to compensate for this if they can only adjust their rate of shoulder rotation. Finally, consistent with the "variability-overuse hypothesis" we looked at in Chapter 2, it is possible that freezing degrees of freedom and moving in the same way with each execution could increase the chance of injury because the performer is always putting the forces onto the same body parts.

But there is good news! Freezing is only the first stage in the model of skill development proposed by Bernstein. The second stage involves "freeing" degree of freedom: the athlete gradually lifting any restrictions they have placed on their movement (e.g., not rotating around the elbow joint) to incorporate more degrees of freedom into their solution. An example of this freeing can be seen in Figure 9.1. Here the server is using their shoulder, elbow and wrist with relatively independent motions for each. So, instead of the rigid coupling we saw in Figure 2, the body parts are rotating around the joints are different rates and in different planes. This allows for much more variation in the serve (e.g., different directions and spin on the ball) making the server much more capable in adapting to changes in the constraints.

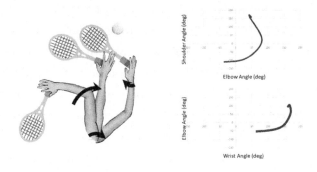

Figure 9.1 – Freeing degrees of freedom. The performer is controlling the tennis stroke with a combination of independent shoulder, elbow and wrist rotations.

Research across a wide range of sports has shown that performers do typically follow this freezing-freeing progression when learning a new skill. This has been quantified using two different measures. For freezing type I (not moving body parts), the primary measure that has been used in the Joint Range of Motion. The basic prediction is that if Bernstein's freezing to freeing progression is what occurs then the joint range of motion should be larger after training as compared to what it was at the start. For the second type of freezing (rigid coupling between parts), the main dependent measure that has been used is a joint cross correlation. This is a measure of the similarity between the time series of two joint angles during a movement, with a value of 0 indicating the increase/decrease in angles is occurring independently and a value of 1 indicating they are changing perfectly in-phase (like our drum sticks back in Chapter 6). Thus, again if Bernstein's hypothesis is correct, we should see a high value of cross correlation at the start of training, with this value moving towards zero post-training.

Evidence consistent with freezing type I has been found in studies of simulated skiing, soccer, and racquetball[1]. In each of the studies, joint range of motion was low at the start of training then increased with more practice. Evidence consistent with the freezing type II pattern has been found in studies of skiing, soccer and darts. An example from a study of soccer by Hodges and colleagues[2] can be seen in Figure 9.2. When the single participant in this case study first started practicing a soccer chip shot over a barrier, they self-organized into a freezing solution as can be seen by the increase in the cross-correlation between their ankle and knee. But with more practice, these degrees of freedom were freed and correlation approach zero.

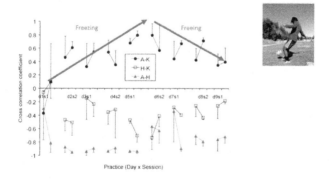

Figure 9.2 - From freezing to freeing degrees of freedom. From Hodges et al. (2005).

So, in sum, if the athlete you are working with self-organizes into a freezing solution it can be good in the short term but, at some point, we need to vary the constraints in practice to encourage them to "free" themselves and find a better one.

The search for optimality

The final stage in Bernstein's model involves the performer finding their optimal movement solution. That is, the one that will allow them to achieve as close to their maximum performance outcomes (e.g., highest combination of accuracy and speed) as possible. Traditionally, of course, what is optimal has been defined in terms of the ONE correct technique that all elite performers share. As we saw in Chapter 3, this has spawned a business of using training methods that seek to give a lesser-skilled performer THE one ideal, expert solution. Before looking at alternatives, let's look at couple examples of attempts to do this.

Research on eye movements in sports has shown that in most sports one of the keys to being successful is looking in the right place at the right time. A typical result found in this research area can be seen in Figure 9.3. While novice baseball batters seem to shift their eyes around randomly all over the pitcher's body, more skilled batters adopt a clear, systematic gaze pattern[3]. That is, they shift between a small number of key locations (e.g., from the pitcher's shoulder to their elbow to the ball release point). So, can we improve an athlete's performance by just training them to adopt the expert's gaze pattern? Well, yes and no. Attempts at training novice performers to adopt a specific pattern (look here, then there) have mostly been unsuccessful. For example, Klostermann and colleagues[4] attempted to train novice beach volleyball players to adopt the gaze pattern of expert players by superimposing red cueing dots on a video showing an opposing team playing the ball. Three groups were compared: a functional group that was trained to adopt the expert gaze pattern (look at the attacker than the anticipated point of hand-ball contact), a dysfunctional group that was trained to adopt a completely different pattern (just follow the ball), and a control group that received no training. Results revealed that participants did not learn to adopt the functional control pattern (their gaze was no different after training than the control group) and there were no differences in performance between the groups. However, it has been shown that use a more simplified training in which novices are only taught to keep their eyes as still as possible before moving (the so called, "quiet eye") can be effective[5].

Expert Group   Novice Group

Figure 9.3 – Eye movements in baseball batting. From Kato, T., & Fukuda, T. (2002).

Similar results have been found when novices are given training to move their bodies in the same way as experts. For example, the robotic assistance of movement. Believe or not, the equipment shown in Figure 9.4 is designed to improve your golf swing not to take over the earth in some science fiction movie! The device, called the RoboGolfPro, is a large robotic arm that attaches the middle of the shaft of a regular golf club. The player stands in front of the robot and swings their club like on a practice range. The robot adds forces during the swing movement in order to alter the length, speed and plane of the swing in different ways – in particular, it can make the golfer's swing follow the trajectory of a pro golfer. In other words, the robot is giving them THE correct movement solution about how to swing. Research using devices like these for golf and for other sports like rowing has shown that while it does lead to change in the movement pattern there is no evidence of transfer of training[6]. That is, after the device is taken away, athletes trained this way do not perform any better (and in some cases even worse) than a control group that received no training.

Figure 9.4 – Robo Golf Pro swing trainer.

So, if we can't just give a performer the optimal solution by showing it to them or guiding them through it how can we help them find it?

. . .

Optimality as Adaptability: Developing Motor Synergies

First off, in our new alternative way of looking at skill acquisition we need to change our definition of what it means to be "optimal". All learners have their own intrinsic dynamics and individual constraints. And the constraints imposed on our movement solutions are continuously changing over time. Given this, there is no ONE ideal movement solution for all performers or even ONE solution that will always be optimal for each individual performer. Instead, we need to think of optimality in terms of adaptability. *An optimal movement solution is one that optimally satisfies the current constraints imposed on an individual performer.* In other words, performing at a level close to one's maximal potential relies of being able to alter one's movement solution in the face of changing constraints.

This is idea is captured nicely in Bernstein's concept of dexterity. As evidenced in the Nadal quote I keep harping on about, being skillful does not involve executing a movement formula drilled into our head through repetition. As Bernstein said: "dexterity is not confined within the movements of actions themselves but is revealed in how these movements behave in their interaction with the environment, with unexpectedness and surprises". Being a skillful mover relies on adaptive problem solving.

In Bernstein's view the key to reaching this adaptive optimality, which occurs is the third and final stage of his learning model, is developing what he called *motor synergies*. Think again for a second about the problem of what to do with your elbow and shoulder when serving a volleyball. In Figures 4.4 and 4.5 above, we saw a couple different ways the degrees of freedom in movement can work (or not work!) with each other in this situation. We can lock one body part like our elbow so that it does nothing at all and place the burden of control on our shoulder. Or we can make it so these two body parts used in our movement solution do exactly the same thing – simplifying the problem but not really taking advantage of our available degrees of freedom. Or, we could just have the two body parts do completely different, independent things such that the cross correlation goes down to zero, like we see in Figures 9.1 and 9.2. While these movement solutions all allow us to perform the task with some degree of success, they will never be optimal. Optimality requires that we move or body parts in a manner such that they work together in synergy.

A motor synergy is a movement solution for which there is functional co-variation between the degrees of freedom that serves to stabilize the performance outcome. Imagine that I am doing an overhand volleyball serve that involves rotating around my shoulder and elbow joints. I throw the ball up in the air, get distracted by an opponent's movement, and start my shoulder rotation a bit later than usual. Or maybe I am outside playing beach volleyball and a gust of wind comes up after I toss the ball such that it is falling faster than I expected. What can I do in these situations? If my shoulder and elbow joints are rigidly coupled or are working completely independently, not much. The combined shoulder and elbow rotation will not be fast enough to get my hand to the ball in time. But what if instead, the rotation about my elbow joint depended on the rotation about my shoulder joint. So, for example, if my shoulder rotation were moving my hand too slowly, I could detect that, and make my elbow rotation faster than normal. Viola, problem solved! Having degrees of freedom that co-vary, working together in synergy so that the value of one depends on the value of the other, allows a performer to adapt to changes in constraints like an opponent's movement and wind. I can achieve consistent, stable performance outcomes (hitting the ball at the right place and time to make an accurate serve) by exploiting this motor synergy.

In my baseball training study, which I discussed in Chapter 4, I found that developing these motor synergies was one of the main things that changed in the group that showed the greatest performance improvements. Recall, that in this study, the VR group that faced greater variability in practice conditions (pitch types, speeds and locations) showed the greatest performance gains. They did better on tests involving hitting in the VR and off a pitching machine, they had better hitting stats in their next full season, and a greater proportion of the batters in the group were drafted into professional baseball. Why did this group improve the most? Figure 9.5 shows part of the answer. In the study, we used force plates on the ground so that we could detect when the batter shifted their weight or lifted their foot on the ground. In the figure you see some of the data we collected[7] – the time at which the batter's lead foot landed back on the ground after the first step (Landing) and the time between this landing point and the start of the actual bat movement (Landing-Swing). Each dot shows one swing made by a batter in the VR group. There are three things I would like you to take from this. First, batters are clearly not executing ONE repeatable swing – the timing of Landing the lead foot on the ground is varying substantially from swing to swing. Second, there are clear motor synergies. When the batter lands a bit earlier than normal, they wait a bit longer to start their swing. When they land a bit later, they start it earlier. These two degrees of freedom in movement are working together, compensating for each other, to stabilize the performance outcome (getting the bat to the right place at the right time). Finally, if we compare the top and bottom panels in this figure, we see that these synergies got tighter and stronger after training.

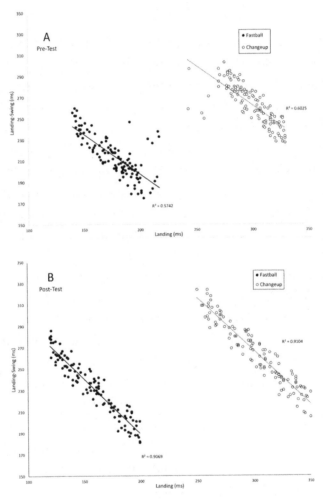

Figure 9.5 – Motor synergies in baseball batting.
From Gray, R. (2020).

An important point to emphasize about these powerful motor synergies is that they could not possibly occur if I were just reeling off a pre-programmed movement I had stored in my head after hours and hours of repetition. Using my elbow movement to compensate for my shoulder movement or adjusting when I start my swing based on when I land requires regulating my movement continuously while it happens. Remember this is exactly what we saw with Bernstein's blacksmith in Chapter 1. Developing motor synergies gives a performer ballistic missiles. They also help us answer one final question related to how effective a movement solution is: how do I distinguish good from bad variability in movement?

Along the manifold: Good vs bad variability

In my baseball batting study, there was considerable variability in the timing of the landing of the batter's front foot that increased after training. In the tennis studies we have been looking at in the last few chapters, experienced players have considerable variability in how much they flexed their knee and in the location of racquet-ball contact. Bernstein's blacksmith had variability in the hammer path. Hopefully, we are convinced by now that variability is not noise to be removed but rather an essential part of skill. But how do we separate the good from the bad? How do we know whether the changes in execution from attempt to attempt are beneficial? To answer this question, let's build ourselves an uncontrolled manifold!

Imagine that you are given a task of pushing down on a surface with two hands such that the total force you produce is 10 Newtons (N). Figure 9.6 illustrates the solution space for this task – all possible combinations of the degrees of freedom (in this case, the force in each hand) that could be used as a movement solution. Just like with any task, not all these solutions are going to work. The solid black line shows combinations that will keep the total force at the goal of 10N – ranging from all the force in one hand or the other to having an equal force of 5N in each. Now, let's say you start with the equal force solution. Any movement or change in your solution that goes along the black line (which we call the "uncontrolled manifold") is potentially *good variability* because it allows you to maintain the goal performance outcome (10N) with different solutions. Why is this a good thing? Well think instead of a task that involves applying force upwards --- carrying a tray of drinks across a busy restaurant to your friends. Moving along the manifold is good because it allows you to keep the tray from tipping when you must squeeze through a bunch of people by holding the tray up in the air with one hand, do that thing with your elbow where you open a door, or shift when one hand starts to get tired. Movement in this direction is good because it makes the performer adaptable to changes in the constraints.

Figure 9.6 – Solution space for a task in which the performer has to push down on a surface with a total of 10N of force.

Now let's consider another change in our solution: from the equal force 5/5 solution to one in which there is 4N in each hand. This change, which we call orthogonal variability because it is a movement in a direction 90 degrees away from the manifold, is *bad variability*. It is destabilizing the performance outcome and making us unsuccessful in achieving our goal. Changing our solution in this manner would result in a lot of broken glass on the floor we would need to clean up! So, here we have our answer. When a performer shows variability in their movement solution it is good when it keeps the performance outcome stable and successful and bad when it does not. This also leads to a key prediction: becoming skillful should involve a relative increase in good variability and a decrease in bad variability with practice. Let's look at some studies that have tested this idea.

Figure 9.7 shows some more data from my VR baseball batting study. In the top panel, I have split a baseball swing into two parts: (i) the time between the ball being released by the pitcher and the batter shifting weight to the back foot and (ii) the time between the back-foot weighting and the bat reaching the hitting zone. From this we can create a time constraint that the batter's movement solution must satisfy. In order to get the bat to the ball, the two times shown in the figure must add up to the time it takes the ball to get there from the point of release. For an 85 mph pitch this constraint would be 479 msec. This then allows us to do a type of uncontrolled manifold analysis. Any combination of the two times that add up to 479 msec represent good variability. This is illustrated in the figure by the thick black line with the shaded pink area showing the margin for error for keeping the ball in fair play. Any change in the movement solution that results in a combination of times substantially greater or less than this constraint is bad variability because it is going to result in the swing being too early or too late to hit the ball successfully.

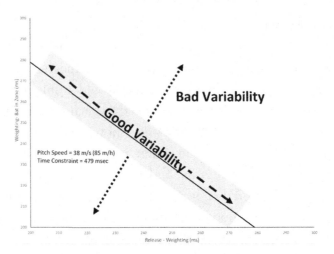

Figure 9.7a (i) the time between the ball being released by the pitcher and the batter shifting weight to the back foot and (ii) the time between the back-foot weighting and the bat reaching the hitting zone.

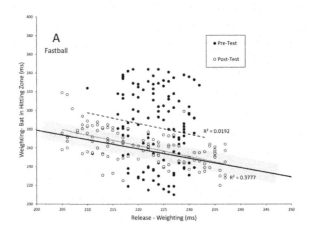

Figure 9.7b Swings made by batters in the VR training group before (black dots) and after (white dots) training

What did I see in my baseball study? The bottom panel in Figure 9.7b shows swings made by batters in the VR training group before (black dots) and after (white dots) training. Prior to the six weeks of training, batters had more bad variability than good: the majority of the black dots fall outside the shaded area. With training this changed dramatically but not in the manner expected from the traditional repetition-based view of skill acquisition. Before training, the batters had a relatively large amount of inherent variability in the timing of the swing which in turn was associated with poor performance – not hitting the ball very often. But this wasn't remedied by eliminating all variability and producing a highly repeatable swing. Batters in my study improved not by reducing all movement variability to as low as value as possible. Instead, they *restructured* the variability – increasing the amount of good (moving along the time constraint) and decreasing the amount of bad (moving away from it). Across all batters in my study, those that had a larger increase in good variability from pre-post training had significantly more hits in both the real and virtual batting tests and had a higher on base percentage in their next full season of play. Similar results have been found in for other sports tasks like throwing[8] and golf[9].

So, in sum, there are clear ways to evaluate the effectiveness of a movement solution but critically it depends on performer's skill level and amount of experience. Initially a "good" solution is one that can get you on the court and playing with some level of confidence and proficiency. This may involve sitting in the local minima we saw in Chapter 6 by freezing degrees of freedom. But to reach a level of self-optimality, the athlete we typically need to explore other movement solutions which involve the development of motor synergies and an increase in good variability. It also may, in some cases, lead to them something that no one has ever done before.

10

A NEW PERSPECTIVE ON WHAT IT
MEANS TO BE CREATIVE

When people talk about creativity in sports one of the first examples that always gets cited is the Fosbury Flop. At the 1968 Olympics in Mexico City, Dick Fosbury famously won the gold medal by going over the high jump bar head-first with his back facing it. At the time, this was a completely new and unique movement solution. All other competitors (or mostly all – more on that in a second) used variants of one of two techniques. Clearing the bar with the side (called the "western roll") or going over it face down (called "the straddle"). How in the world did Fosbury come up with this highly creative movement solution that was clearly not just an adjustment to an existing technique but rather a completely new pattern of coordination?

Figure 10.1 – The Fosbury Flop and The Brill Bend

The traditional view of creativity is that it is a passive, cognitive process. It starts with an individual sitting down and coming up with different ideas about how to do something. If creativity had a logo, it would be Rodin's The Thinker. In our business model analogy, creative ideas are generated by the boss and the cognition department. The role of the motor control department is only to execute these new ideas once they have been passed down from above in a new memo or mission statement. Acting is not part of creativity; it is the subservient expression or realization of it. But is this really the case? Let's return to the story of Dick Fosbury.

I ask again: how did Fosbury come up with the idea of doing the flop? Was he just sitting on a bench one day going through different movement options in his head, watching other competitors go over sideways and face-first, and then suddenly, eureka: I going to go over backwards! No. The story of the Fosbury Flop suggests that there were other important factors. First, right about the same time Fosbury was coming up with the flop there was a change in the equipment used in high jumping. Specifically, sand and sawdust pits which provided little cushioning if you landed the wrong way were replaced with the high-density foam mats you see today. Or stated using the terminology I have been pushing throughout this book, there was a major change in the *task constraints* imposed on Fosbury and other high jumpers. And what do changes in constraints do? The encourage exploration of different movement solutions. The second point to emphasize is that Fosbury's college coach at Oregon State, Benny Wagner, was somewhat unorthodox. While most of their practice involved the traditional approach of trying to repeat the one correct technique (Wagner's preferred technique, the western roll), at the end of every practice Wagner also encouraged Fosbury to try a couple jumps in which he just improvised. Even after Fosbury started doing the Flop, Wagner had him continue to practice both techniques. In other words, his coach created an environment that included some degree of variability and allowed for exploration.

But perhaps the most important part of the Fosbury story that changes how we think about creativity is the fact that another person came up with exact same solution at the same time. About 300 miles up the coast, in Langley British Columbia, a young high jumper named Debbie Brill started doing what her coach dubbed, "The Brill Bend" – going over the bar backwards just like Fosbury. In 1970, at the age of 16, she would use her newly developed technique to become the first North American female to clear six feet in the high jump. By all accounts the two had never met and it is very unlikely that Brill would have ever seen footage of Fosbury practicing in late 1960's. So, how did they both come up with the identical, highly creative solution? If creativity is primarily a mental process, did they have some kind of thought transference?

If we look at Brill's comments[1], we can see the much more reasonable, alternative answer to this question. First, according to Brill: "There was no way anybody was going to land on their back in sand or sawdust," "It would be too self-destructive." "But when I saw the foam mat for the first time, I decided to try something different". Clearly, the change in the task constraints was as, if not more, important for the creative process as any internal, cognitive process. Also, like Fosbury being inspired by his coach to try something different, Brill, who did not have a coach when she first started, was known for exploring different ways to get over the bar (including doing a tuck and roll or using a scissor kick) even before she came up with The Brill Bend.

Creativity does not involve an individual first coming up with an idea in their mind and then sending it down to the motor control department to execute. Acting is not simply an expression of creativity. It is a central part of the creative process. Creativity is not an asymmetric process, occurring within the head of an individual then pushed out to the environment like a new product. It arises from a symmetrical, coupled interaction between the individual, task and environmental constraints faced by a performer. Traditionally, we could call Dick Fosbury and Debbie Brill, "creative people", reflecting the view that the creativity all came from the individual. While it is very likely that both had individual constraints that supported creativity (a willingness to try new things and fail at times), what was happening in their environment around them (the constraints imposed by equipment and coaching) was equally important. Creative solutions are not ideas. They emerge when a performer is acting and searching for solution to satisfy the constraints of a task. The symbol for creativity should not be the thinker, but rather the explorer!

Further evidence in support of this alternative view of creativity can be seen when we look at more of the factors that seem to be related to it. If, as traditionally assumed, creativity is primarily a mental process that involves generating new ideas than it should be related to our memory abilities. Specifically, being able to hold more things temporarily in your working memory so that they can be compared and combined in new ways should allow for greater creativity. In 2019, Orth and colleagues[2] performed an interesting test of this idea by first splitting a group of 42 kickboxing novices into low and high working memory capacity (WMC) groups. To do this they used a WMC test similar to the one you can try for yourself[3]. They were then asked participants to perform two tasks simultaneously: (i) strike a target on the left hand-side of an instrumented heavy bag such that the force was above a threshold level that was chosen to be challenging for each participant and (ii) memorize a series of digits that was playing over a loudspeaker, like if someone was saying their phone number to you. This digit task was used to take up some of the participant's working memory with the main prediction of the study being: participants with a low WMC should come up with fewer creative solutions for striking the bag because they have less working memory available to come up with new ideas in their head.

But how do you measure creativity in a movement skill like this? For a solution to be creative it requires two things. First, it must be functional. A crazy idea that does not lead to a performer achieving their goal is just a bad solution, not a creative one. In the Orth et al study functionality was defined in terms of force. That is, a solution was functional if it generated a force that was at least 90% of the target given to each participant. The second, more important, feature of a creative solution is originality. Like the Fosbury Flop or Brill Bend, it must be something rare, something no one else is really doing. What might this look like in kickboxing? While the most common solution is just to punch the bag with your dominant hand, participants could also use their other hand, strike with their feet or elbows, start with back to the bag and use a backhand motion, spin and strike, or really any type of motion they wanted. They were told that they had to stay within the square area marked on the floor and hit the left-side of the bag but also: "you may use this space in any way you wish, and you can strike the bag with any part of your body ". In the study, the researchers classified all the different solutions used and defined an original solution as one that occurred less than 5% of the time across all participants.

What did the results of this study reveal? There was absolutely no relationship at all between working memory capacity and creativity, or performance for that matter. On average, the high working memory group came up with five creative solutions while the low working memory group came up with six. On average, the success rate was 35% for the high WMC group and 43% for the low WMC group. Not only are these differences not statistically significant, but they are also in completely the wrong direction. They are also exactly what we would expect over here at Self Organization LLC. As we saw in Chapter 3, when we measure an ability like working memory capacity using a test like the one in the link above, we are modularizing functions and taking them out of context. So, we expect them to have little if any connection to perform a skill like kickboxing.

So, if it is not general perceptual-cognitive abilities like working memory capacity that determine creativity than what does? Consistent with what we saw in Chapter 6, further analysis of the kickboxing data revealed that creativity seems to be related to how a performer searches the perceptual-motor landscape. Specifically, the number of creative solutions generated in the study was related significantly to two search factors. First, where the participant started in their search. Because participants were asked to hit the left side of the bag, there was a natural attractor for the task to strike with the left hand. This is obviously the most efficient and shortest path to the target. However, because all participants were right-handed, this was not likely to be the solution that could generate the most force. In the Orth et al study, it was found that participants that started striking with their left hand on the first attempt produced fewer creative solutions (that are both forceful and original) than those that started striking the bag with something other than a simple left-hand jab. On the surface this seems a lot like the Tim Tebow problem. When you start with a solution that has a strong attractor but is not optimal (due to your intrinsic dynamics) it makes it more difficult to pull away and search for a new one. If we were coaching the participants in this study, we would likely want to constrain the task in some other way to de-stabilize the left-hand strike attractor.

The second factor that seems to be related to creativity was, not surprisingly, the degree to which a participant switched between using different patterns of coordination (particularly, those involving the right side of the body). While participants that failed to produce creative solutions spent most of their time trying to persistently tweak their existing solution (e.g., punch at a different angle, or using a different starting position), those that did produce creative solutions were more willing to switch to completely different coordination patterns (kicking instead of punching, spinning instead of straight on, etc.). Creativity comes through acting, searching and adapting to constraints not through have a powerful supercomputer or a boss that comes up with all the ideas.

Embracing the Unorthodox

Another commonly cited example of creativity in sports is the greatest cricket batsman of all time, Sir Don Bradman. Relative to his peers, Bradman is arguably the greatest athlete of all time. His career batting average of 99.94 runs per inning is roughly 50% better than any other batsman in the game. For comparison, the career recorder holder for batting average in baseball, Ty Cobb, is only 2% higher than the 2nd place batter. What made Bradman so exceptional and why has no one been able to repeat it? Again, supporting the problems with looking at skills in the traditional modularized and de-contextualized way, Bradman was dismissed from the Australian Army for having defective eyesight. A study at the University of Adelaide found that his reaction time (measured by having him press a button when a light came one) was slower than that of an average undergraduate student. Instead of having better general perceptual-cognitive abilities, his success is attributed by most to his unorthodox rotary batting technique, which is described in detail in an excellent article by Renshaw and colleagues[4]. This technique allowed Bradman to have quicker bat speed through the striking zone as compared to conventional hitting solutions.

How did he come up with this solution? Was it given to him by coach? Did he sit and think then just start doing it? No! Just as we saw with Fosbury and Brill, it was largely the result of a change in the constraints. Bradman spent a lot of time practicing a game he invented on his own – batting a golf ball around in his basement as it bounced around off a water heater. Using a smaller ball reduces the margin for error for successfully striking the ball. Hello, change in task constraints. Hitting the ball of a round surface like a water heater is going to cause unpredictable and erratic bounces that must be played. Hello, variability of practice. Bradman's creativity came from his self-imposed exploration of the movement solution space.

All these examples raise an important point that comes from our new way of thinking about skill – as coaches, parents, instructors and athletes we need to be more accepting of different ways of doing things. Becoming good at something does not require conforming to some ideal solution. It involves adapting to the constraints you are faced with – some of which, critically, are your own individual constraints. We need to let performers explore, try things out and let them find solutions that work for them. Clearly, giving this kind of freedom was central in the examples of creativity we have looked at in this chapter so far. Fosbury's coach encouraged him to do a few attempts that were different. When he came up with the extremely unorthodox method of going backwards over the bar, his coach did not tell him to stop it and do it the way I know is best. He asked him to practice it both ways. For Debbie Brill it was persistence and the strength to not worry about what others thought: " When I first started, I was all gangly and awkward," "It wasn't at all gangly and awkward when I was the best in the world." Finally, one can only imagine what might have happened if a traditionally minded coach or parent had walked down into Bradman's basement and told him to stop messing around and do "proper" cricket practice. So, if we are not going to suppress creativity, individuality and exploration, let's start to look at ways we can encourage these things..

How do we promote creative movement solutions?

To start, let's look at how some of the coaching methods we have been discussing serve to support creativity. In Chapter 7, we saw how manipulating constraints through small-sided and conditions games can encourage athletes in sports like soccer, basketball and hockey to explore new movement solutions. Does this method also help to promote creativity? This question was addressed in a recent study by Caso and van der Kamp[5]. Video recordings of soccer practice were broken down into small sided game activities (e.g. , 5 vs 5 or 6 vs 6) and compared to practice using full 11 vs 11 games. Similar to the kickboxing study, the authors defined creative behaviors as one's that were effective in achieving the goal and occurred less than 5% of the time across all the actions categorized. Examples of creative actions found in the study including passing with chest, kicking with the outside of the foot, and performing a "Maradona turn". How did the practice design influence the emergence of creative actions? Well, there was a very clear pattern – five creative actions were seen in 5 vs 5 games, three in 6 vs 6, two in 7 vs 7, and none in the 11 vs 11. Having fewer players on the ball, which alters the space and time available to play the ball and amplifies information about interpersonal distance, seems to encourage players to explore a wider range of movement solutions leading to increased creativity.

A similar pattern of results can be seen in studies of differential learning. In a study by Santos and colleagues, 40 soccer players were split into two training groups: one involving traditional prescriptive training and a differential learning group. For the latter group, random perturbations in the practice conditions were added including changes in the player surface (e.g., turf vs natural grass), shape of the field (e.g., rectangular vs circular) and type of ball (e.g., a rugby ball vs a soccer ball). Creativity was assessed using the Creative Behavior Assessment in Team Sports tool which, like the other studies we have already looked at, assesses both the functionality (did the pass get to the attended receiver?) and originality of actions. What was found? Following five months of training, the differential group produced actions that were rated as more versatile, original and creative.

An example of using the CLA to promote creativity can be seen in the study of dancing by Torrents-Martin and colleagues[6]. In this study, the body movements of three pairs of contemporary dancers were compared for two different instructional constraints: "When dancing, try to keep your pelvis as close as possible to your partner" or "when dancing, try to keep your pelvis as far away as possible from your partner". While the first instruction led to a stronger coupling between the dancers the second led to greater exploration. Specifically, the dancers began to add other movements like walking and jumping to the performance. Notice, again there are no explicit details given about how to move here. The experimenters were not choreographing the routine for them. Instead, with the second instruction, they asked the performers to produce a behavior that is very different to what they normally do (not staying in contact for a type of dance that requires it) which led to greater exploration of movement possibilities as compared to the instruction that reinforced existing tendencies.

So, not surprisingly, coaching methods which encourage self-organization, exploration and variability are also those that seem to inspire creativity. In the CLA, changes to the constraints faced by the performer are invitations to explore the perceptual-motor landscape with variable movement solutions. In differential learning, performers are asked to execute tasks in (sometimes bizarrely) different ways than they ever have before. In both cases, this increased movement variability should increase the likelihood that the performer will come up with something that is creative (i.e., rare and adaptive).

Next, we will continue to look at ways we can practice skills that inspire creativity along with fun, confidence and a love of movement by focusing on the important issue of youth sports coaching.

11

YOUTH COACHING: THE PROBLEM WITH CONES & MAKING PRACTICE FUN AGAIN

I started this book by lamenting the types of practice I saw kids doing as I walked through the park. The problem with the way we traditionally coach youth sports can be summed up in one word for me: cones! If you played soccer as a kid, you were no doubt subjected to the ubiquitous practice drill of dribbling a ball through a line of cones. Your coach likely told you that doing this was critical for learning "ball handling technique", that it would improve your "agility" and that you had to learn "fundamentals" like this before you can start playing the game. But imagine if you faced the equivalent of a line of cones in a real game. Imagine that you are on a break-away, dribbling the ball towards the goal with a chance to put your country ahead in the waning minutes of the World Cup final. You see that there are a bunch of orange candy wrappers laying on the ground in a line in front of you. What would you do? Would you move from side to side, using your "agility" and "ball handling technique" to go in and out of them? No, of course you wouldn't! You would run straight over top of them!

. . .

The problem here is that skills like "agility" and "ball handling" are functional and driven by information from the environment. But they are not being practiced that way. As an attacker you go left with the ball because the defender is leaning right or moving towards your right side in attempt to steal the ball from you. You are deciding what to do and acting using information from your opponent's body posture and movements. These movements have a purpose – getting around a defender, avoiding losing the ball, etc. We don't cut right or left when running, dribbling, or puck handling just for the fun of it. When we dribble around cones there is no information that we can couple our actions to. Referring back to Chapter 5, a cone is an abstract cue with no inherent relevance to it, not the type of information Gibson purposed we used to control our actions. There are no affordances. There is no decision making required of the athlete. All we have is a prescribed instruction from a coach telling us what to do. It is fake agility.

There are other problems too. In order to dribble around the cones, the player must look down at the ground. Is that really what we want them to be doing? If a hockey player is taught stickhandling a puck like this, they are likely to have rude and painful awakening when they do it in a game. Finally, dribbling around cones requires the athletes to stand and wait in a line for their turn to go. For many kids all they have been able to do all week is play with a ball by themselves in their backyard. Now, they finally get to a practice field with a bunch of other players they can interact with and they…have to wait in line to play with the ball by themselves. Insert sad trombone sound.

. . .

It has long been assumed in traditional coaching that teaching skills to novices must start with *task decomposition*. That is, we need to take a perceptual-motor skill and break apart into its fundamental components, isolate them, and then have an athlete repeat them over and over. Then and only then can we put the components all back together and let the athlete play the game. Along with dribbling through cones, there are numerous other ways we do this in youth sports coaching. Hitting balls off tees in baseball, running through "agility" ladders or tires in football, hitting balls tossed underhand by a coach in tennis, practicing the ball toss in volleyball serve without striking it, doing passing lines in basketball, etc. For all these practice activities we have removed the purpose of the action. The athlete is doing it only because they have been told to by their coach, not because it helps them to achieve some goal, realize some affordance. In all these drills, we have broken the natural coupling between information and action. The direction we dribble or run or pass a basketball depends on how our opponents and teammates move. Timing a baseball swing or a tennis forehand requires picking up information from the flight of the ball. In all these drills we have removed all decision making from the athlete. They are moving where the coach told them to go (go left around the cones, pass to the player across from you), swinging at every ball or, in some cases, not even acting at all.

In my opinion, the flawed assumption that we must decompose skills and teach the fundamentals before we play the game is killing youth sports for many. Isolated, decoupled practice activities like the ones I have described are boring and just not very fun. They remove all individuality, exploration and the creativity we saw in the last chapter. They are forcing one ideal movement solution on kids that have different individual constraints and intrinsic dynamics. When kids struggle to master the "fundamentals" in sports training or PE class they drop out of sports. They do not get the chance to further develop their joy of movement, express their own perceptual-motor skill and movement creativity, and grow a love of actively interacting with their environment. Instead, they learn that they are "uncoordinated" and "not sporty" and move on to something else. There must be a better way...

Keep 'em coupled: Task simplification not decomposition

So, we need an alternative way of reducing the complexity of sports to make it easier for kids to acquire the necessary perceptual-motor skills. Let's put our heads together and see if we can come up with an alternative practice activity other than a line of cones. We want kids to learn to coordinate the movement of their feet, while keeping their eyes up, and deciding which way to go based on information they pick up from the movement of the person they are interacting with. Can you think of anything? Too late! As kids we already figured this out ourselves over 150 years ago! The answer is playing tag. The game of tag is functional and purposeful with the participants trying to realize clear affordances (tag someone else or get away). It is coupled and information driven. They only way you are going to successfully tag someone is by regulating your movement based on the perceptual information from the other person's movement. It involves a ton of decision making. Lunge at them no or try to force them to move in that direction. And there is a reason it has been played by kids for so long – it is fun!

. . .

There are various ways that tag can be adapted for soccer practice[1]. Having a coach try to tag players while they keep control of a ball. Having two players control a ball within a designated area with one trying to tag and one trying to keep away. And there are many others. No lines. No kids standing around doing nothing. No looking down at the ground. No isolated movements kids could have done by themselves in their backyard. No fake, un-purposeful agility.

In the new way of thinking about skill acquisition the preferred method for reducing the complexity of sports for new learners is *task simplification* instead of decomposition. In task simplification, the whole movement is always completed. Movement and information always coupled. To make the movement easier for a new learner we *scale down* the skill while always trying to keep its basic structure. For example, we could play tag in soccer or football to train agility instead of dribbling through cones or running through tires. Tag simplifies the problem of control (I only need to focus on one player) while not breaking it apart. We can reduce the pitch speed or move the pitcher closer instead of hitting off tees in baseball. As I will dive into detail more in a second, we can reduce the size of the equipment (e.g., lower the height of a basketball hoop) instead of doing soft toss or passing lines.

The two keys here are that: (i) we want to allow the performer to develop the same type of information-movement coupling they will use for the full skill and (ii) we want to make sure that we still have some degree of variability in practice conditions so that the performer learns to solve movement problems. We want kids to learn to coordinate their movement and make decisions based on the information they will use in the game, right from the start, not learn isolated movements and then try to plug it into the game later. Before getting to more examples, let's look at some more of the problems with the traditional "learn the fundamentals" approach.

The dangers of decoupling perception from action

Along with the problems I have already described, there is another major limitation with using task decomposition, in particular when it involves decoupling perception from action. There is a growing body of evidence to suggest that we perceive the world differently when we are required to act on it as opposed to when we are not. And how we act is very specific to the perceptual information available. Let's look at a few examples.

In a study published in 2010, Dicks and colleagues asked experienced soccer goalkeepers to perform a series of different tasks while viewing an opposing player taking a penalty[2]. The gaze behavior of the goalkeepers was measured using an eye tracker. Results for two conditions of particular interest here are shown in Figure 11.1. The white circles in the top three panels show the eye movements that occurred in a *decoupled* condition in which the keeper was not required to act but rather was asked to just say the direction the kick was going ("right" or "left). The bottom three panels show the same keeper's gaze behavior in a *coupled* condition in which they had to try and dive to stop the shot. Clearly the keeper is using a completely different gaze behavior strategy in the two conditions. I found a similar effect in a study where we asked participants to either judge the direction of or try to catch a simulated approaching ball[3]. No matter what feedback we gave, participants continued to make small errors in judgements (saying the object was going off to side more than it really was) but when we let them try to catch it, these errors disappeared, and their hand went to the right place.

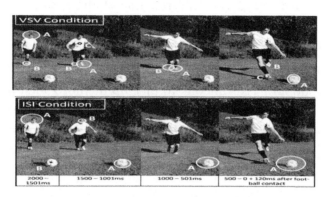

Figure 11.1 – Gaze behavior in uncoupled (top) and coupled (bottom) goalkeeper tasks. From Dicks et al. (2010).

Effects like these are also consistent with what we know about the way visual signals are organized in your brain. After light hits your eyes and is converted into an electrical signal it travels to the back of your head, arriving at an area called the visual cortex. From there it splits off into two paths. The dorsal stream going to the brain areas in the top of your brain and the ventral stream going to areas in the bottom. Why split in two? Well, as purposed by Goodale and Milner[4] these two areas seem to be doing "vision for action" and "vision for perception" respectively. That is, one is using visual information to help guide actions while the other is using it to allow for passive perception and verbal responses. Evidence in support of this division comes from patients with brain damage who can do one of these things but not the other. For example, a patient studied by Goodale and Milner named

DF struggles to verbally indicate the orientation of a line (e.g., whether it is "vertical" or "titled right") but has absolutely no problem putting letters into mail slots with different orientations. It is also the case that many visual illusions (e.g., the Muller Lyer illusion shown in Figure 11.2) trick one of these systems but not the other. Most people will say that the horizontal line in top part of Figure 11.2 is longer than the horizontal line in the bottom even though they are the same length. But, if you build this figure out of wood and ask someone to pick up the horizontal part, the distance between their fingers when they reach to grasp it will typically be the same in both conditions[5]. So, the bottom line is: when you ask an athlete to perform a decoupled task where they are perceiving without acting they will be using different parts of their brain (the "vision for perception" ventral stream) than they will use when they actually play their sport.

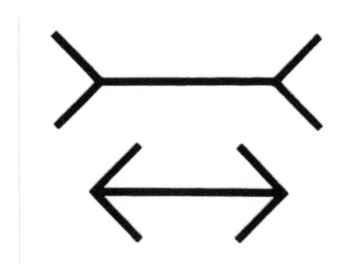

Figure 11.2 – The Muller-Lyer illusion

A similar problem comes when you ask a performer to act but you do not include the information they normally use. For example, research on cricket has shown that hitting off a pitching machine, which removes the information a hitter gets from the bowler's body language and delivery, results in different patterns of movement (in particular, how they step forward or backwards to meet the ball)[6]. Anecdotally, some highly skilled cricket batsman and baseball players struggle to hit off a pitching machine even though they are some of the best in the world at the far more difficult task of hitting off a real bowler or pitcher.

But perhaps my favorite example of this is the story of Jennie Finch vs Albert Pujols. Jennie Finch was one of the most successful softball pitchers of all time (2 time All American and Olympic Gold medalist) while Albert Pujols has had a hall of fame career as a baseball batter. In 2004, the year he faced Finch, Pujols had a .331 batting average, hit 46 homeruns, and was selected to the National League All Star team. Surely, just using a bigger ball, moving the mound a little closer and having the pitcher throw underhand shouldn't really affect a highly skilled batter like Pujols. But you can see the results for yourself here [7]. He did as well as you or I could do. In three pitches he did not once even make contact with the ball never mind getting a hit.

The key point here is that being skillful relies on a performer developing a highly specific relationship between the information in their environment and their movement. When we break this relationship apart by de-coupling perception from action it fundamentally changes the nature of the task the athlete is performing. This makes it much less likely that there will be transfer of training. For example, Pujols' many years of practicing hitting a baseball didn't seem to transfer at all to hitting a softball. And, as illustrated in the examples we have been discussing, decoupled training is typically isolated, repetitive and, well, just not very fun. So, let's look in more detail at one of the most well studied alternatives: equipment scaling.

Scaling equipment

Imagine for a second you are an 8-year-old of average height (about 50") trying to learn to play tennis. You are instructor hits a looping shot over the net that they want you to return with a forehand stroke. Houston, we have a problem! According to the International Tennis Federation, tennis balls should only be used in play if they have a bounce range between 53 and 58" inches. Along with the challenge of hitting a ball that is likely to go over your head, you have to do so with an adult tennis racquet that is 27" long, which is longer than the length of your arm. Not surprisingly, research has shown that in this situation, youth tennis players tend to hit the ball with relatively low velocity and accuracy, contact the ball behind instead of in front of their body, do not have the desired low to high ("rainbow") stroke path we discussed in Chapter 7, and are generally more passive and less confident. The problem here is that the interaction between constraints (the task constraints of the racquet and ball size and the individual constraints of the player's size) lead to the emergence of a highly ineffective movement solution. So, how can we improve this situation? While the traditional approach has been to decompose the task (e.g., having the young player hit balls that are tossed underhand by a coach standing close by so the ball doesn't bounce as high), recent research suggests that equipment scaling is a far superior method.

Instead of fundamentally changing the task the young athlete is trying to perform by decoupling it, the task is simplified using lower compression balls (25% of a regulation adult ball) and smaller racquets (21" instead of 27" in length). Research by Tim Buszard and colleagues has shown that these changes lead to several highly beneficial adaptations to the player's movement solution[8]. For example, in a study published in 2020, 25 youth tennis players completed 10 strokes with adult equipment and 10 strokes with scaled equipment while their body movements were tracked. Along with differences in performance (players were significantly more accurate with the scaled equipment), there were major differences in how the swing was coordinated. Referring back to ideas we looked at in Chapter 9, when they used the adult equipment, participants seemed to primarily use a freezing strategy. They controlled the stroke by varying the upper arm while keeping their forearm relatively frozen. When using the scaled equipment, motor synergies (or functional couplings) emerged with the movements of the forearm being strongly correlated with the movements of the upper arm. In other words, using the scaled equipment allowed them to *free* degrees of freedom and come up with a more effective movement solution!

Similar results can be seen in other sports. For example, using lighter basketballs for practice with 10-year old's resulted in greater shot accuracy and higher ratings of self-efficacy (the belief that one will be successful in achieving the task goal) as compared to training with regulation balls[9]. After completing 16 practice sessions using a lighter than normal volleyball, 7th graders had higher set and overhand serve accuracy during match play[10]. In a 2016 paper, Buszard and colleagues[11] reviewed a total of 25 studies investigating equipment scaling for sports tasks including tennis, basketball, volleyball, cricket, throwing and catching. They found that for 18 of them there were significant performance benefits as compared to training with standard, adult equipment. In sum, appropriately scaling a sports task for the individual constraints of the athlete seems to be a highly effective training approach that avoids the problems associated with the traditional practice of breaking the skill apart. And which would you rather do? Hit soft lobs tossed to you by a coach into an empty court? Or be given different equipment that allows you to engage in a rally with an opponent?

But do kids learn "the fundamentals" by just playing games?

One question that I often get from coaches when discussing the use of task simplification methods like scaling equipment and small-sided games is: but do the kids learn the fundamentals if we just let them play the game instead of doing isolated drills that focus on technique first? Before tackling some of the problems with this question itself, let's look at some research that has addressed it. In a 2017 study, 10-11 year-old soccer players completed 22 weeks of practice involving small-sided games[12]. They were not given any traditional, technical instruction but instead the goal was for them to learn skills like dribbling and passing "in the game". Before training, at 11 weeks, and at the end of training, dribbling and passing skills were rated on a scale from 0-2 by a group of experienced coaches. These were based on things like whether the pass was too hard or too soft, led the intended receiver appropriately, and whether control of the ball was maintained. While there were not improvements from 0-11 weeks, there were significant improvements in both decision making in execution of the skills by the end of training. This seems to be consistent with what we see when we use other types of manipulations that encourage self-organization in practice like increasing variability. While it may take a bit longer for the basic skills to emerge, in the long run athletes develop the same "fundamentals" we see in traditional isolated training.

A more important question is should we be even worrying about this at all? What exactly is a "fundamental" anyways? The concept comes from the long-accepted assumption that there are basic building blocks that we must put together to become skillful, like the example shown in Figure 11.3. But this idea suffers from the same problems that we have been discussing throughout this book. It assumes a linear, deterministic relationship between fundamental movement skills (if we want Skill 1 we just add Fundamentals A, B and C) that is not consistent with what we seen in an adaptive complex system like an athlete. We are back to our old business model. It fails to recognize that skills are highly specific to the information available in the environment. Like we saw with dribbling around cones, in most cases "fundamentals" lack purpose and are not functional. They are just aesthetics, not really achieving any goal other than producing the movement itself.

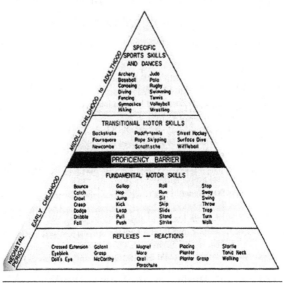

Figure 4 — Adapted from Seefeldt (1980) Pyramid taxonomy of fundamental motor skills.

Figure 11.3 – Pyramid taxonomy of fundamental motor skills. From Newell (2020).

My favorite way to illustrate this latter point is a story that James Rudd from LJMU conveyed to me when I interviewed him for my podcast[13]:

"One of the skills on the assessment battery, which is often used is something called a gallop. Like a horse where one leg stays behind and the other comes forwards. I'd demonstrate it for you, give you a practice and then I'll ask you to do it twice. So I'm going to look at how rhythmic your movement was. Does one leg overtake the other leg? Do your arms kind of move in his pendulum motion? So, I'm looking for this kind of template of a movement.

I remember this one girl and she couldn't get it. It's quite common to be honest. They can't get started. They can't do it.

So, I said, don't worry. You did wonderful. Thank you very much. 10 minutes later, it's break time. So, I popped outside and I was watching her group playing on hill in their playground. And I'm watching, they're playing this game of chase and then she's chasing one of the other children and she starts running down this hill. And what pattern comes out perfectly from this: the gallop!"

Executing this weird running motion out of context, without a goal, has no purpose other than satisfying the examiner. It has no function. It affords nothing. It is another example of fake agility. But put the person in a task with a specific goal (notice we are back to playing tag) then it has a purpose (keeping balanced when running down hill) and a performer finds the solution. If a movement pattern like a gallop is functional, if it is needed to achieve some goal for a specific task, it will emerge when we perform that task. There is no experimental evidence or solid rationale to support the idea that it works the other way around, where we teach fundamental building block movements in abstract and then have you piece them together into skills later.

Another problem with concept of "fundamentals" is how they are evaluated and assessed. This is typically done in a very circular manner. The coach who spent weeks trying to get the athlete to move in one particular way or teach them to make this decision for this particular play is the one assessing their technical and tactical proficiency?! No wonder why we see a lack of creativity in a lot of sports. It is also the case that when we assess "fundamental movement skills" we are looking for a *convergent* solution. Can the child solve this movement problem in this specific way? But this does not fit at all with this new view of skill as involving adaptive, variable, problem solvers. What we want to see are *divergent* solutions: how many different ways can you achieve this goal?

Specialization, Diversification and Donor Sports

One takeaway we might get from all of this is that kids should always be practicing under conditions that are highly similar to and representative of their sport. Conditions that have the same information, involve the same type of gaze behavior, movements, etc. In other words, this alternative view of youth coaching seems to fall clearly on one side of the specialization vs diversification debate in youth sports. Specialization is a must to be skillful. But this is not the case.

An interesting new concept in youth sports training is the *Donor Sport*[14]. Within this approach, and consistent with ideas of adaptability and problem solving we have seen throughout this book, it is proposed that athletes need to become versatile and adaptive movers before they can become expert athletes. Furthermore, they need to become attuned to affordances (that is, opportunities for action) in sports performance contexts. The key to becoming an adaptive mover and this attunement is the use of so-called donor sports which emphasize exploratory practice and guided discovery. Donor sport activities are ones which share some of the same athletic movements and affordances required for successful performance in the athlete's primary, target sport.

As an example, consider training for the primary sport of soccer using the donor sport of parkour. For those that don't know, parkour involves moving from one point to another (using a variety of jumps, summersaults, running, rolling, etc.) through a complex unstructured environment. Again, we have been doing this for years as kids in playgrounds. Why could this help a young soccer player? Because the two share some of the same affordances. For example, a sidestep maneuver needed to drive past a defender in soccer shares some of the movement skills and coordination dynamics and involves a similar affordance (obstacle avoidance) to moving around an object in parkour. It also involves some similarities in the perceptual information (distance and time to contact with obstacles and the size of gaps between obstacles) used to guide the action. So, in theory (these ideas still remain to be tested in research studies), practicing parkour should result in positive transfer of training to soccer performance for young athletes. One of the main reasons parkour is championed (as opposed to some other movement based sport like gymnastics, diving or figure skating) is its open and exploratory nature. Because the athlete is not following instructions to perform a prescribed set of movements that have a specific form, it is more likely they will develop skills adapted to the constraints of their own intrinsic dynamics leading to, again in theory, better transfer of training.

Another reason why it is important for youth athletes to diversify their training and not focus solely on their own sport is that it can lead to in a change in their individual constraints resulting in improved performance when they do go back to their main sport. Increased strength, flexibility, speed, etc. It can also lead to increased *body awareness*. As we saw in Chapter 7, it is common for performers to be insensitive to the information about their body position provided by their internal senses (proprioception and kinesthesis) because we are used to relying on visual information so heavily. But research has shown that educating our attention to this information can be important for performance.

In 2015, Han and colleagues[15] conducted a study looking at 100 elite athletes (all competing at regional, national, or international level in China) across five different sports: gymnastics, swimming, sports dancing, badminton and soccer. There was also a control group of 20 non-athletes. Body awareness was measured using a technique in which the athlete's body parts are positioned at different angles with a mechanical device and they asked to indicate the angle while blindfolded. This ability, called proprioceptive acuity, was measured at five body sites: the ankle, knee, spine, shoulder and fingers. What was found? For all body sites and for all sports, acuity was significantly higher for the athletes than the non-athletes. Within the athletes, level of competition was significantly correlated with acuity scores for the ankle and shoulder but not for any of the other body locations. Using this data, the authors constructed a multiple regression model to try and predict sport competition level based on acuity scores and found that they could explain 30% of the variance in level based on proprioceptive ability alone. So, there seems to be some evidence that higher level athletes are more sensitive to information about body position. Finally, there was no significant relationship between the number of years of sport specific training and proprioceptive acuity suggesting that we don't develop sensitivity to this type of information from traditional sports training. Instead, the best way to develop it would seem to be to encourage young athletes to participate in donor sports focusing on form and body positioning.

. . .

To sum up the problems with the traditional way we coach young athletes, I will leave you with the words of PE teacher and researcher Ken Alexander[16]:

"I assert that many school programs keep three 'dirty little secrets' from those outside the profession: They (the kids) struggle to develop motor skills, they don't develop game performance and they don't develop fitness. Apart from that – all's well."

What we are doing is not working. It's time for a change!

12

WHAT ARE WE "ACQUIRING" ANYWAYS? THE NATURE OF EXPERTISE, AUTOMATICITY AND DIRECT LEARNING

B efore I return to more practical implications, I want to address the question: what changes when we become highly skillful? What makes someone an expert in their sport? In the traditional view of motor learning, expertise has two key components: through practice we (1) acquire knowledge that (2) removes the need to focus our attention on the control of our actions. The first component is captured in the term we use to describe what happens in training: "skill acquisition". With practice we *acquire* things that are stored in our brain: representations of our environment that allow us to compute and predict, the motor programs we discussed in Chapter 3 that allow us to repeat our movements, memories of events that we can use to interpret the new situations we might face, etc. Much as we saw with the traditional view of creativity, skill is something that we possess – it comes from within the individual.

The second component of skill in the traditional view is reflected in the strong emphasis that has been placed on *automaticity*.

Becoming automatic through training has been held with the same regard as our old friend repetition and they two are typically thought to go hand in hand. For legendary UCLA basketball coach John Wooden, "The importance of repetition until automaticity cannot be overstated"[1]. Norman Peale emphasized that:" repetition of the same thought of physical action develops into a habit which, repeated frequently enough, becomes an automatic reflex"[2]. For Celtics player Bill Sharman: "It's a game of habit or repetition. It's a reflex. The game is so quick you don't have time to think."[3] Within the traditional view of skill, thinking about or paying attention to what you are doing is a burden that must be lifted. This is why we have long called them practice *drills*. Borrowing from the military, the idea is that we want to train you in practice (following the same repetitive path as a drill bit) so that when you are in the heat of competition skill execution becomes reflexive, habitual and automatic.

Is this really what it means to be skillful? Is our goal in practice really to become disconnected from our environment so we can just run off automatic programs or routines? Let's look at how the nature of expertise has been recast in the skill revolution.

Skill adaptation not acquisition

What is the difference between Ronaldo and Ronald? To understand the alternative account to the acquisition/automaticity concept of skill, I want to begin by breaking down this wonderful testing session in which soccer legend Ronaldo attempted to play in the dark[4]. In the test, Ronaldo is playing balls crossed in front of the net under conditions in which the lights are turned off at different points. While he seems to be able to handle this situation quite well (for example, making a solid header into the corner when the lights are turned off at the point the kicker strikes the ball), the lesser skilled patsy in the video, Ronald, struggles.

The typical explanation given for why Ronaldo can do this is the internal model he has acquired through years of practice. According to the commentators in the video: "By 500 msec Ronaldo's subconscious has interpreted Andy's body language, worked out what direction the ball will go in, *calculated* its speed and trajectory, and then *programmed* his body to reach it at the optimum moment" and "it's almost as if he is doing math in his head.". As we can see, the two traditional components of skill are here. His ability to play the ball skillfully depends on internal model (computer) he has acquired that allows him to calculate and predict. After he stops computing, the model outputs are sent to the motor control department so an action can be programmed and executed without the need for any further processing (i.e., automatically).

Why have we long thought that expertise works this way? I like to use this Ronaldo video because it highlights a key assumption of traditional theories of skill acquisition. That is, that the information we pick up through our perceptual systems is somehow insufficient and impoverished. When Ronaldo is looking at the player and the flight of the ball, there is not enough information there for him to control his actions successfully. What he is perceiving needs to be interpreted, processed and enriched by the computer in his head for him to be successful in scoring a goal. This, of course, only gets exacerbated when we turn off the lights and take some of the perceptual information away.

· · ·

This *indirect* view of perception is something that James Gibson did not like, not one bit! In his view, it was completely unnecessary and overly complicated. As we saw in Chapter 5, through analyzing tasks like pilots landing plans and people walking through cluttered rooms, Gibson found that there was information available in the environment that could be used to control actions without needing to do any additional work. Perception could be *direct*.

And this is the case in the Ronaldo video, even when the lights go out. Figure 12.1 illustrates the case of a soccer player moving to intercept a crossed ball. The traditional assumption is, of course, that for interception to be successful the player needs to predict where the ball is going and when it will get there, then generate some sort of movement that will get their body to the predicted location at the predicted time. But surprisingly, all this is not really necessary. You don't actually need to try to predict *where* and *when* to be successful in your goal. Why? Because as Gibson illustrated, there is direct information that you can use to achieve your goal. Specifically, in this situation, these is an angle (β in figure 12.1) created between the player and the moving ball. If the player moves so that she/he keeps this angle the same (e.g., speed up if it starts to get bigger, slow down if it gets smaller), they are guaranteed to arrive at the right place and time. End of story. But what about when the lights go out? Well, that's fine. If the player just keeps moving in the same way they were when the lights were on, and nothing changes about the flight of the ball (which it doesn't in this testing) they will still successfully intercept it. For those that might be interested, my full analysis of all of the plays in this Ronaldo/Ronald test can be found here: https://perceptionaction.com/ronaldodark/

. . .

So, let's look again at what makes the player skillful in this case. If through practice, the player learns to use the "constant bearing angle strategy"[5] illustrated in Figure 12.1, which by the way is also used by a host of other animals ranging from dragonflies to fish, what exactly have they *acquired*? They are not really computing or predicting anything. They are not relying on stored memories of plays they have made in the past. They are just adjusting their movement in response to information from the environment. They are *adapting* to their environment, establishing a beneficial relationship with it, not acquiring something from it that allows them to be disconnected from it.

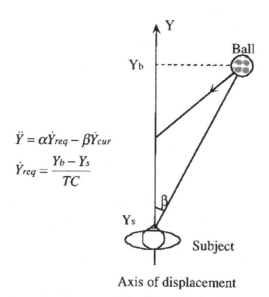

Figure 12.1 – Intercepting an approaching ball
through information movement coupling. From
Chardenon et al. (2002).

Direct Learning

"Learning is about attending to things, rather than acquiring the knowledge that absolves us of the need to do so..." – Tim Ingold[6]

So, if we are not acquiring anything, we are not building up our internal models or computer software, what exactly is happening when we come more skillful? As illustrated in the wonderful quote from Tim Ingold, learning is not about creating an asymmetry where we separate ourselves from the environment, stop paying attention to it, and run off internal programs. In the skill revolution, expertise is all about building a stronger, more effective connection with our environment. More specifically, as proposed by Jacobs & Michaels in their Direct Learning theory[7] illustrated in my infographic in Figure 12.2, there are three types of changes that can occur as we learn and become more skillful.

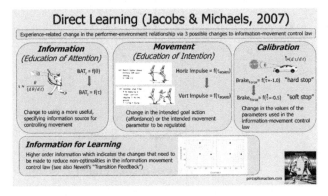

Figure 12.2 – Direct Learning Infographic

The first change is we can control our movements using better, more effective sources of information, in a process called *education of attention*. To illustrate this let's look at learning to drive. Like about 2/3 of the world's population, I learned in a country (Canada) where people drive on the right side of the road. This made it quite a challenge to drive on the left when I moved to England in 2010. For me, driving on the left was a very conscious, demanding process. I had to keep reminding myself stay on the left and think very carefully about which way I looked to check for oncoming traffic when making a turn. This example is a clear case of *negative transfer of training*, where something I learned before makes it harder for me to learn a new thing. But imagine for a second, that when I learned to drive, I was traveling back and forth between England and Canada regularly to visit relatives. It is very likely that I would have educated my attention to a more effective information source allowing me to drive in both countries. Specifically, because the steering wheel is on the opposite side of the car in the two countries, a much more effective control rule is: drive so that your body is always positioned in the middle of the road near the center line.

Educating attention involves a switch to using information that is more effective for the control of action. What Gibson termed *specifying* information. It typically allows a performer to achieve their goal in under a wider range of conditions. Using the car's position on the road as an information source only works in one or the other country (or, at least, it must be relearned when you switch). Using your body's position works for both without any adjustment. Another common example occurs when people learn to control collisions, for example when trying to create one in baseball batting or avoid one when walking a busy road. We have found that when people first start performing these tasks, they often use the object's distance as the information source to control their action (e.g., swinging when the ball is a certain distance away, and thinking it is OK to cross for cars that are far away)[8]. With practice, particularly under conditions in which the object's approach speed is varying and the distance strategy is no longer effective, they switch to using the object's time to collision as the information source.

These findings can be linked back nicely to our discussion of constraints and the CLA in earlier chapters. The information source a performer uses to control their action is strongly influenced by the constraints present in the practice environment. If they practice only under very restricted conditions (learning to drive only in Canada or hitting off a pitching machine set at a constant speed) they are likely to educate their attention to a less effective information source. This is again another reason why we don't want highly repetitive, low variability practice. We need to vary the constraints to encourage performers to educate their attention to more effective information. We will look at some specific examples of how this can be done using visual constraints in the next chapter.

The second change that can occur when we learn a skill is *education of intention,* when a performer changes their goal for their action. This can occur both at a high level where the overall goal is changing and at lower levels. An example of the former could be a soccer defender starting with the goal "just keep the attacker in front of me" to have a more specific goal like "push them into my teammate", "try to steal the ball", or "make them go to their weak foot". At lower levels, a performer can have the same overall goal but change the aspect of movement that intend to control to achieve it. We saw this in my golf putting study I discussed in Chapter 7: with experience, golfers shift from regulating the speed of their back stroke to regulating its length when putting from different distances.

. . .

Another example can be seen in the sport of long jumping. One of the keys in to achieving a long jump is to be able regulate your run up to the board so the jumper hits it at a high speed without going over it. In the seminal study by Lee and colleagues[9], it was shown that long jumpers seem to do this by adjusting the length of their last few strides using a visual information source that specifies their time to collision with board. But what parameter of the movement do they control to create different stride lengths? At this point, you should hopefully not be too surprised to learn that there are multiple ways you could do this. Hello, Bernstein's degrees freedom problem nice to see you again! It can be achieved by varying the horizontal reach of your stride (called horizontal impulse), how high you lift your legs vertically (called vertical impulse), by leaning more or less, etc. Studies looking at the effects of skill level on long jumping performance have shown that one of things that seems to change with experience is which of these parameters is used to control stride length[10]. For example, many athletes seem to switch from controlling it via horizontal impulse to altering vertical impulse with increased practice. This is a better strategy because it does not require the athlete to take into account the speed they are travelling when making adjustments.

The final thing that can change as we become more skillful is the *calibration* between the information and our movement. A good example of this many of us have experienced again occurs in driving. When we buy a new car or rent one, it is common to discover that the brakes don't quite work the same. But after a couple sudden, hard stops or near collisions we quickly adjust and start braking smoothly and normally. What's going on here is *re-calibration*. We are still controlling the same aspect of our movement (the force generated by our foot on the pedal) using the same information (the time to collision with the car in front of us) but we have changed the relationship between the two. If the brakes are a bit spongier, we need to push a bit harder as the time to collision gets shorter. If they are a bit tighter, we need to push with less force.

For all three of these learning processes, we do not need to infer some internal processing or computation inside the performer's head. All that is occurring is change in the relationship between the performer and their environment. A change in what they are picking up from it, a change in the aspect of their movement they are coupling to it, or a change in the calibration between these two. And although they may seem like relatively simple changes, research has shown that they can provide very powerful explanations of behavior.

A great example of this can be seen when we look at the task of navigating through a cluttered environment. Imagine you are in a shopping mall, and you see a friend. But between you and them are other shoppers, kiosks, fountains and a host of other obstacles. How do you control your behavior in this situation? The traditional explanation is that you use an internal representation (a kind of mental map) of the world to plan a route through the objects to your goal. But does it have to be that complicated? Do you really have to determine the locations of all the objects in the environment before you can act? Does the boss have to send a planned route to the motor control department before they can do anything? As shown in an excellent series of studies by Fajen and Warren[11] the answer is: "no". What if we just stared walking without planning anything? Instead, we establish a relationship between an aspect of our movement (the rate at which you turn your body as you walk) and an information source (the angle to our friend and the angle to the obstacles). Research has shown that using this information-movement control law not only gets you to your goal with bumping into anything, but it also produces routes that are highly similar to the ones people actually use.

So, in sum, the control of actions can be explained much more simply, more parsimoniously, as the establishment (and adaptation) of information-movement control laws in which the performer directly picks up some action-relevant information from the environment and uses it to regulate their actions. No need for prediction, information processing or assessing memories of previous actions.

Do we really want to become automatic?

As we saw in Chapter 3, in the traditional business motor of skill acquisition, learning occurs through distinct, linear stages. The most influential model of this type is this one proposed by Fitts and Posner in 1967[12], illustrated in Figure 12.3. In this model, when we first start learning a new skill, we use controlled processing. That is, we recall how you have been instructed to position our different body parts, holding these steps in our working memory, and focus attention on our body to determine if the positioning is correct. So while making a golf putt we would be consciously going through the steps: "Align shoulder, hips and knees parallel to the target", "grip the club with thumbs pointed straight down.", "Position eyes directly over the ball", etc.. But, if we keep practicing and practicing, we can reach the other end of the acquisition spectrum, called automatic processing. Put simply, being automatic means that you can perform an action without thinking about the execution of the movements involved. A term that you will often hear in association with automaticity is that of "muscle memory". This is used to represent the idea that control of the movement no longer requires attention and conscious control. Instead, through practice, expert performers essentially develop internal routines or programs for executing the movement. Once the routines are activated, they can run pretty much on their own. But is this really what happens?

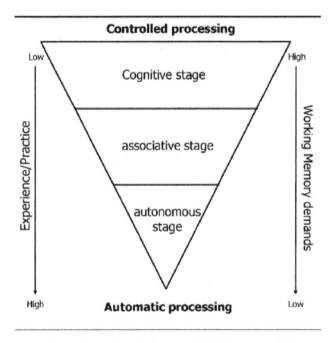

Figure 12.3 – Fitts & Posner (1967) Model of Skill Acquisition

Proponents of this new skill revolution don't think so[13]. In the traditional view of skill acquisition, becoming automatic involves no longer using things like memory retrieval, selective attention, a linear set of steps used to act, top-down control from an executive controller and working memory. At Self-Organization LLC none of these things were thought to be involved in the control of action in the first place! Even if we take a more general definition of automaticity as being a less effortful, more routine type of skill execution I don't think it really has much meaning in the new view of skill either. If we really believe that skill involves adaptability and having multiple movement solutions, then the effort involved doesn't really lessen with experience -- it just of a different type. Skillful behavior is not rote, repetitive and automatic. It is adaptive, responsive and intelligent. We want to develop skills not just habits..

Skills vs habits

Habits are rote behaviors in which each manifestation is (at least an attempt at) a mere replication of its predecessors. Habits are acquired through drills or conditioning and involve little intelligence. When we describe someone as doing something by habit, we mean that they do it automatically and without having to mind what they are doing. Habits do not typically involve care or vigilance. They are fast and reflexive. By contrast, when we talk about doing something skillfully an element of intelligence is involved. Skill involves sensitivity to one's circumstances and may require the performer to do quite different things on different occasions. And if we believe Bernstein's argument – something slightly different on every occasion. Put more succinctly, skill involves innovation, whereas as habits involve sheer repetition. Habits are pre-formed motor programs while skills are more adaptive and flexible.

Another key difference between the two is the role of improvement. When we talk about skills, we (at least hope) that at

some level the performer is being critical of their behavior ---
they are identifying poor outcomes, figuring out ways to improve
and monitoring their progress. Each execution of a skill should
hopefully modify its predecessor – the goal is to improve through
practice. By contrast, we do not practice habits in order to
improve them. This is like what we might also distinguish
between a skill and a routine.

Do we want performers to develop habits or skills? Obviously, by
the way they are defined here, this is a bit of a loaded question.
Of course, we want skills. Skillful behavior is intelligent and
reactive to changing constraints both in the short and long term,
involves an element of improvement, is concerned with the how
–whether or action is conducive to achieving our goal. But think
about it – aren't a lot of the ways we currently coach developing
things that are closer to habit? Aren't we often teaching our
athletes and students inflexible, repetitive responses?

13

THE EVOLVING ROLE OF TECHNOLOGY AND DATA IN SUPPORTING SKILL DEVELOPMENT

I n sports, we seem to have a never-ending appetite for gizmos and gadgets that claim they can improve our performance. Sports training technology is an industry that continues to grow rapidly, in most cases vastly outpacing the research on which it is claimed to be built. No more is this exemplified than in the sport of golf where there are numerous types of clubs, balls, mats, braces and, as we saw in Chapter 9, even robots designed to help take a few shots off a round. Recently this trend has been supplemented with technology that can provide us with more and more data about our performance. GPS sensors that track position, mats which measure force, Blast monitors that measure ball flight and spin, phone apps that analyze our movements and provide biomechanical data, etc. and so on.

Not surprisingly, the way in which technology and data are mostly used in sports training has followed the traditional approach to skill acquisition. "Brain training" devices which seek to improve general perceptual-cognitive abilities like response speed and attention using a modularized, context-independent approach. Technologies and data designed to "correct" your movement and get it closer to the ideal pattern. As we have seen in previous chapters, research has provided very little support for the idea that training this way leads to positive transfer of training. So, let's look at some alternative ways training technologies and data are starting to be used, to instead support exploration for movement solutions, perception-action coupling, and self-organization.

Manipulating Visual Constraints

As we saw in Chapter 12, a key to become skillful is learning to use more effective information from our environment – educating one's attention. In many ways the use of information by a new learner is like the concept of attractors in movement coordination. Often a performer will get stuck using one particular source and, as a coach, you need to somehow push them away from it so they can explore other information. A good example of how this can be achieved are technologies which constrain the vision of an athlete.

Chin Up Goggles (shown in Figure 13.1 and the video here[1]) were developed by Ed Coughlin and colleagues at the Cork Institute of Technology in Ireland as way to use the CLA in practice for sports like soccer, basketball, and hockey. They are basically a standard pair of sport goggles with a small piece of plastic at the bottom which blocks the lower part of an athlete's visual field. The purpose of using these googles is right there in the name – encourage the athlete to keep their *chin up*, instead of looking down at their feet, stick, or ball/puck they are dribbling.

By adding this constraint, the hope is that they will educate their attention to visual information from the positions and movement of other players, etc. that can be used to perceive affordances and aid decision making.

Figure 13.1 - Chin Up Goggles.

The effects of training with these googles was investigated in a study recently published by Dunton and colleagues[2]. In the study, 15 experienced male soccer players were trained to receive, control then pass a soccer ball to a target. Players were split into either a group that used the Chin Up googles or a control group that practiced normally. Because one of the goals of the occlusion training was to educate attention to information in the external environment, the authors added an interesting twist in the form of a dual task design: in pre and post training tests participants were asked to receive and pass the projected ball while at the same time calling out numbers that were projected on a screen in front of them that changed every half second. What was found? The group that wore the Chin Up goggles had a significant decrease in passing errors (from 5.2 to 1.4 on average) and in number callout errors (from 32 to 9 on average) while there were no significant changes for the control group. So, in other words, the addition of this constraint both improved ball handling and the ability of the athlete to pick up information from the external environment.

. . .

Another example of this approach can be seen in the temporal occlusion glasses used in a series of studies by Raoul Oudejans and colleagues[3]. These glasses contain liquid crystal which can be activated with a remote electronic switch, allowing the experimenter to completely block the athlete's vision at any point during the action. In their studies, Oudejans et al used a practice condition in which the glasses were closed at the start of a jump shot then opened when the ball was above the line of sight. The purpose of adding this constraint was to get the athletes to utilize visual information later in the action, which the authors' previous work had shown that this was critical for accurate shooting. In one study a group of six players from the national under 21 leagues in the Netherlands completed eight weeks of training using these occlusion glasses. Following training, they looked at the hoop a little bit longer (by about 20 ms on average) before releasing the ball and had an associated increase in shooting percentage both in lab tests (from 57 to 63%) and in the game (from 35 to 49%). In another study published in 2012, Oudejans and colleagues found similar benefits of occlusion training for wheelchair basketball players[4]. In this case, participants drove under a large screen that initially blocked their view of the basket. As soon as they saw the basket they shot, again encouraging use of late visual information. The screen training resulted in a significant increase in shooting percentage in on court tests.

A final example of a sports training technology that can be used to encourage an athlete to explore different sources of visual information are stroboscopic glasses[5]. Like the occlusion glasses used in Oudejans' basketball studies these can be open and closed electronically. However, they are not used to block a specific part of the action or a specific part of the athlete's visual field. Instead, the glasses open and close at a set frequency creating an effect like a strobe light in a dance club. You can see, then you can't, you can see, then you can't. For me, using this technology aligns nicely with the differential learning approach discussed in Chapter 8. Instead of trying to take away a particular information source like in the CLA, we are adding random fluctuations to the practice environment to create stochastic resonance. So far, the results from training studies using stroboscopic glasses have been mixed with some showing transfer of training to performance when the glasses are removed and other studies finding no such benefits[6].

Virtual Reality

Virtual Environments, in which a performer can interact with some simulation of a real environment, offer great potential for supporting the approach to skill acquisition I have been promoting in this book[7]. Adding constraints and variability to practice can often be difficult to achieve practically. Changing constraints like the size of the field in a small-sided game, the speed of a baseball pitch, the height of a net all take time to implement so can be difficult to use when practice time is limited. Another issue in "real" training is that it can be difficult to individualize practice for different athletes, making sure the level of challenge and difficulty is appropriate for each. Finally, in "real" training it can sometimes be difficult to remove constraints in a way that ensures the change in movement solution they produce is "sticky". If we suddenly take a constraint like a connection ball or cues from a coach away, it can often lead to the performer reverting to their old solution. Fortunately, all these issues are relatively easy to address when we supplement real training with virtual training.

. . .

As examples, we can look at a few of the training studies I have done in my baseball batting VR. In the study I discussed back in Chapter 4, I was not using the virtual environment to simply recreate and do additional reps of what was happening on the field. I used it do something that is difficult to do in the real practice, and that was based on well-established principles of motor learning: adding variability to practice and challenging each batter at their own level. In separate studies, I have found similar effects when training batters to increase their launch angle[8] (i.e., hit balls in the air more) and hit the ball to the opposite field[9]. Training for these involved using virtual barriers as constraints that the batter had to hit the ball over or not allow their bat to touch during their swing. One of the advantages of doing these things in the virtual environment was that I could move the position of the barrier based on their performance and make it fade out at the end of training. For me, the results of these studies suggest that the greatest value of using virtual reality as a training tool for sports is not the ability to create more repetitions of the same types of practice that are used in real training. Instead, the biggest return on investment for developing a sports virtual environment is likely to come from the ability to create unique, evidence-based training conditions that are impossible or highly impractical to use in real training. Value added not replacement.

Self-optimization through biomechanical modelling

As we saw back in Chapter 6, the fact that there are substantial differences in the intrinsic dynamics and individual constraints from athlete to athlete means that there is no ONE correct movement solution that is going to work best for every performer. This suggests that we need to rethink the way biomechanical analyses of athletes have traditionally been used. In a typical analysis, an athlete is brought into a lab, fitted with motion sensors and asked to perform several repetitions of a sports movement (e.g., throw 10 fastballs at maximum effort). Consistent with traditional thinking about skill acquisition, data from these assessments has typically been used to identify "flaws" (i.e., deviations from the ideal) and provide an athletes or coach with this information so they can make "corrections". An example of this can be seen in the study published by Glenn Fleisig and colleagues from the American Sports Medical Institute (ASMI)[10]. Forty-six healthy baseball pitchers were given biomechanical evaluations to identify deviations in their mechanics from normative values established from testing on 100 elite pitchers. For example, differences in stride length or the amount of shoulder rotation. So, in other words, comparing an individual athlete to an "average expert" like we saw back in Chapter 1. After each evaluation, the ASMI staff produced a personalized video analysis of the pitcher explaining the flaws detected. These were sent directly to the player or to their team. How many of the flaws were corrected when the pitcher returned for the 2nd evaluation a year later? Of the 138 technical issues that were identified, 61 (44%) were corrected. The relatively low success rate here is not surprising given our new view of skill acquisition as it is not really considering the individual differences in coordination (i.e., the foundation on which the new solution needs to be built).

An interesting alternative to this traditional approach was used in a recent study by Felton and colleagues[11]. In this study, an analysis of a high-level cricket bowler was used to create a biomechanical model relating his joint angles and torques during the delivery to ball velocity at release. Using this, the authors were able to identify changes in movement parameters that could optimize the output for this individual bowler. Specifically, it was found that when greater trunk extension and later shoulder extension were used in the model there was an increase in pitch velocity of 10% or roughly 8 mph. This is a massive effect in a sport where a couple mph increase in velocity can have very large effect on the success of a pitcher. However, a key issue that will need to be addressed in future studies is whether it is possible for the bowler to learn to use this new, self-optimized solution.

Movement sonification

So far most of the examples I have looked at may be out of reach for many coaches and athletes because they can be very expensive and/or require access to a testing laboratory. An example of a cost-effective and easy to use technology that has been used to support self-organization and exploration in sports training is movement sonification. This involves taking some parameter of your movement (like the angle of your knee or the speed or your arm movement) measured using a low-cost sensor attached to your clothes and mapping it on to some parameter of a sound that is being played through a speaker. So, for example, I could make the sound get louder the more you extend your knee or get higher in pitch the faster you move your arm. These sounds are essentially a new informational constraint that provide the athlete with additional feedback about how they are moving. It has several advantages of other types of feedback: it can be given concurrently during the movement, it does not require the performer to take their attention away from critical visual information, and it takes advantage of our sensitivity to small changes in acoustic signals.

. . .

As an example, let's look at the system developed by Boyd & Godbout[12] for training crossovers (putting one foot over the other to go around a corner) in speed skating. The sonification system, which cost less than $500, was comprised of a single elastic sensor that was placed on the shin of the skater and produced a signal related to the amount of ankle flexion. Specifically, if the ankle extension went above a certain threshold the system played a harsh sawtooth tone through a speaker with the tone getting louder the more the threshold was passed. If the skater stayed within the threshold during their movement, a more pleasant pure tone was played.

In a study published in 2010, the authors used this technology to train a skater that was struggling to correct a technical flaw. Specifically, when the skater attempted to put their right skate back down after crossing it over their left skate, they would dig their toe into the ice causing a loss of speed and/or falling. Although this skater had been able to perform successfully in the past (competing at a national level), they had suddenly lost the ability to do this basic maneuver. When they arrived at this testing, they had been working unsuccessfully with various coaches and sports psychologists for 14 months trying to correct the problem.

During the sonification training, which lasted for two months, the system was used in three different ways. In the first part of the training, it was used to provide traditional corrective feedback. A threshold deviation for ankle extension was created based on an expert model and every time the subject went above this value the sawtooth tone was played. The threshold was lowered with each session. This is sometimes called "pull" feedback as it is trying to pull the performer towards the correct technique. The second type of training was focused on awareness. For this, instead of trying to avoid the sawtooth tone, the skater was instructed to try to purposely make it happen. To quote the authors:" The aim was to reduce the threshold until the purposeful extension of the ankle was gone and the athlete, using his new-found awareness of the correct amount of ankle extension, was left doing correct cross-overs". Notice the similarity between this and the method or error augmentation we saw back in Chapter 4. The final type of training was called instruction based. For this, the system was changed from a feedback one to one that provided auditory prompts at instances when the extension should occur during the crossover maneuver, again based on data from an expert skater. Similar to training gaze behavior or robot golf swing training we saw in Chapter 9, the system was now being used to get the performer to adopt an ideal solution.

What was found? Qualitatively the athlete's skating form was much better after the training and they were able to execute some flawless crossovers, something they had not done in months. In terms of which feedback was most effective, the corrective feedback seemed to have the least effect. The authors noted that it seemed to produce very similar results to the prescriptive instructions he had been receiving before in that it led to very deliberate and non-fluent attempts to keep the toe up. The awareness training seemed to be much more effective, and it was during this part of training that the skater executed some flawless put downs. The instruction-based training was also less effective because it required too large of changes from the existing pattern. So, again promoting exploration and self-organization to solve the problem (in this case, by using sound to increase body awareness) seems to be best.

Data and analytics

In my graduate statistics class, I try to motivate students by starting the class with the following statement: "If you are look at the world today there are tons of people measuring stuff (where you go online, how much you walk, your sleep patterns, etc.) but they are a very few people that have even the slightest clue what to do with all of this data. That's where you can come in!". For me, this is no truer than in sports. While organizations are investing heavily in technologies to measure everything and teams of analysts to crunch the numbers, they have often ignored one critical piece: how to pull meaningful metrics out of the data and distill this down to an athlete in a way they can use it. This is and will continue to be a major part of effective coaching.

As an example of the challenge here let's look at a couple more of my studies. In baseball, like in all most every other sport, teams collect tons of information about their opponent's tendencies. What types of pitches does the other team's pitcher like to throw and when do they throw them? Where in the strike zone does that batter get the most hits and where can you get them out? But an issue that it rarely discussed is: how do we present all of this to the players so they can use it? I have witnessed teams that give players small books with scatter plots, pie charts and tables of numbers before each game showing the tendencies of the pitcher or hitter, they will be facing that day. Can they really understand the key trends from that? Can they use it to hit and pitch better? What is the best way to present the data to them?

To tackle this question, I created a simulated pitcher with specific tendencies (for example, they liked to throw a curveball, low and away on 0-2 counts)[13]. I then compared three groups. The first was an explicit instruction group that had access to a season's worth of pitch charts for this simulated pitcher and could study them for 15 minutes before starting the experiment. The second group was the self-discovery group. They were not given the pitch charts at the start, but instead after each at bat, they were shown what the pitcher threw in each count. Finally, there was an implicit group that were given no extra help and just had to learn the pitcher's tendencies on their own over the course of the experiment. What were the results? As you might expect, in the first "game" facing this pitcher, the explicit group that studied all the pitch charts hit better. But this advantage quickly went away. By the 2nd game the self-discovery group was hitting just as well. Although, the implicit group did improve from game to game they never hit as well as the other two groups. This suggests that giving the extra data about tendencies does help an athlete, and if you give them all the information, they show an immediate advantage.

Then I did something nasty. I brought in a new simulated pitcher with completely different tendencies and measured how each group performed. All the groups were given no information about this new pitcher. Not surprisingly, the explicit group had a tough time – their batting performance dropped, and it was clear from looking at the data that it was because they were anticipating the wrong pitches. This is an example of a negative transfer of training effect; learning the tendencies of one pitcher hurt performance when transferring to a different one. But surprisingly both the self- discovery and implicit groups showed no such effect. Both hit the new pitcher well with the self-discovery group doing the best. These findings suggest that providing data about an opponent's tendencies gives a significant advantage to a batter, however, there is a trade-off (between short-term effectiveness and negative transfer) which depends on how the information is presented.

We found a similar sensitivity to how opponent's tendencies were given in a study of baseball pitchers[14]. A common practice in baseball now is to create heat maps for batters which show their batting average for different pitch locations. So, for example, the map might be blue for pitches low and away to indicate the batter has a poor .210 batting average for those pitches and bright red for middle-in pitches to indicate they have a very good .380 average for those. Well, although these displays seem nice, they essentially introduce the possibility of something bad happening— ironic errors. Ironic errors involve doing specifically what we intend not to do. Be it not thinking about pink elephants when we are told not to, hitting a shot right in golf when there is a water hazard on that side of the green, or throwing a pitch inside to a batter who is most effective at hitting pitches in that location. Ironic processes theory predicts that under pressure these "hot and cold zone displays" might induce ironic errors. That is, pitchers throwing the ball exactly where they don't want to.

To test this idea, we asked highly experienced pitchers to throw at images of a batter and strike zone projected on the wall. The strike zone was divided into four quadrants. One quadrant was marked in black which pitchers were told was their target and they would get 1 point for hitting. Another quadrant was marked in red which pitcher were told was a high average location that they should avoid and would get -1 point for hitting. Finally, the other zones were white which they were told they would get zero points for hitting. What did we find? Sure enough, under pressure, pitchers hit significantly fewer of their targets and threw significantly more pitches into the ironic zones. Interestingly, when we looked at movement kinematics the pitchers were not being erratic, they were acting like they were trying to hit the ironic zone. So, one of the recommendations I now give to teams is to give data displays that show what you want your athletes to do (e.g., just a hitter's cold zones to a pitcher) not what you want them to avoid.

Another issue associated with using data in skill training is the potential danger associated with inducing an internal focus of attention in an athlete. With it becoming easier and easier to measure body position or movements, it is very tempting for a coach to just give that information directly to the athlete. For example, telling a golfer that "your arms are too close to your body on your backswing" or a tennis player that their "knees aren't bent enough". In a large body of research spanning over 20 years now, Gabby Wulf and colleagues[15] have shown that directing a performer's attention to their body like this (called an *internal focus of attention*) results in inferior performance and learning of skills as compared to conditions where their attention is directed outwards towards the effect of their movement (e.g., the angle of the clubhead) or something else in the external environment (e.g., the position of your opponent on the other side of the net). One proposed reason why an internal focus of attention may be inferior to an external one is that the former disrupts the self-organization of degrees of freedom occurring in the athlete's body parts. Stated another way, focusing internally leads to you bossing your muscles and joints around which we now know is not how our perceptual-motor system is designed to work. Evidence for this can be seen in studies measuring muscle activity under different focus of attention instructions. An internal focus (on "the arm position" when lifting weight, for example) not only leads to less force generation it also is associated with greater muscle activity, as measured by surface EMG[16]. This greater activity tends to occur when one is consciously focusing on moving a body part.

A similar problem can occur when athletes use some of these monitoring technologies on their own. Yeoman and colleagues[17] compared practicing with or without using a smart phone app on a driving range. The app videoed the swing and could be used to identify specific technical aspects to work. Both groups trained for four weeks. Analysis of training journals revealed the group that used the video app had more than twice as many statements reflecting an internal focus of attention and about 1/3 fewer reflecting an external focus, as compared to the group that training without the app. More importantly, driving accuracy significantly decreased following training for the group using the video app while it increased for the other group.

These self-discovery, ironic error and focus of attention effects all lead to one important conclusion: there needs to be a coach between the data and the athlete! For example, instead of telling a golfer "your hand path is too low" use an analogy like "think about casting a fishing line" to get the desired change in movement pattern. To avoid ironic errors, don't talk about things to be avoided. Be careful with letting an athlete just use monitoring and data collection technology on their own. And, finally, don't overload an athlete with information that may disrupt natural, self-organization.

14

INJURY PREVENTION & ADAPTATION (NOT REHABILITATION!)

I n sports today, it seems like keeping an athlete healthy and on
the field so that they can perform their skill is as, if not more,
challenging than helping they become skillful in the first place.
For example, the rate of ACL reconstruction surgeries in sports
has increased by over 20% in the last 10 years. The number of
UCL (Tommy John) surgeries has been increasing by 6% per
year. One of the most exciting aspects of this revolution in the
way we think about skill acquisition is that it also has great
potential to help prevent injuries and allow athletes to get back
on the field faster when they do occur.

Injury Prevention through Variability

In Chapter 2, I introduced the idea that movement variability
and degeneracy may be an injury prevention mechanism. Being
able to move in different ways to achieve the same goal not only
gives an athlete the advantage of being able to effectively adapt
to the ever-changing constraints they face, but it also has the
potential to reduce the impact and wear and tear on the body

associated with repetitive movements. And what is the best way to tap into this? By using practice conditions which promote it!

In a recent study, Orangi and colleagues[1] examined whether coaching methods which promote variability and movement degeneracy help to reduce risk factors for ACL injuries in soccer players. Sixty-six novice soccer players were split into three groups that trained for 12 weeks. A traditional, prescriptive instruction group was trained using repetitive, corrective practice designed to promote the "correct" techniques for shooting and passing. So, in other words, the coach was trying to minimize the variability in skill execution. A CLA group was encouraged to explore movement solutions using constraints manipulations including the use of small-sided and conditions games. Finally, a differential learning group practiced with random perturbations to the practice conditions including things like which side of the foot they had to kick with, hand positions and type of ball. To assess the injury risk, all participants were asked to perform a change of direction test in which they had to run at full speed to a marker and then cut at 45 degrees. During this test, the researchers used motion tracking to measure variables that have been shown to be risk factors for ACL injuries in previous research. These included things like trunk, hip and knee flexion angle, and peak ground reaction force. What was found? For both the CLA and differential learning group all the measures changed in the good direction (and by significantly more than for the traditional training group). For example, from pre to post training, the knee flexion angle increased, and the magnitude of ground reaction force decreased. These results support the idea that adding variability and exploration to practice serves to reduce the risk factors for injury.

. . .

Injury Prevention through more representative practice design

As was discussed in Chapter 11 when looking at youth sports coaching, a critical factor in effective practice design is representativeness. That is, to what extent are athletes using the same information, performing the same types of movements and looking in the same places in practice as they do in competition? Research suggests this issue of representative design is not only critical for learning the skill, but it also may be important for injury prevention. An important example of this is how unplanned and unpredictable movements are incorporated into practice.

In most sports, it is common for athletes to have to make *unplanned* movements. For example, a football defender needs to cut suddenly when a ball player changes direction. A hockey goalkeeper needs to save a deflected shot. A volleyball player needs to alter their spike mid-air based on the position of the blocker. How well do we incorporate these types of movements in practice? Not very well at all in most cases! As a consultant, one of the comments I find myself making a lot when observing practice activities is: "well that was a nice dance recital when does practice start?". This is not in any way meant to put down the difficulty and skill involved in dance but rather to point out that in most practice drills athletes know exactly what is going to happen. Movements have essentially been choreographed. They know where the tires or cones are going to be that they must go through. When and where the coach is going to hit the ball that they must catch. Etc. Everything is *planned* and predictable. So, even though unplanned movements are they situations in which injuries are more likely to occur we rarely allow athletes to learn to adapt to them.

A recent volleyball study by Mercado-Palomino and colleagues[2] illustrates why this can be problematic from an injury prevention perspective. Twelve semi-pro players were asked to move to block at one of three locations above the net. In the planned condition, the blocking location was given before the run-up was initiated whereas in the unplanned condition it was signaled with lights mounted above the net that turned on after the player's run-up had already started. Ground reaction forces were measured with force plates mounted on the court and a motion capture system was used to capture movement data. What was found? Force place data revealed that power and energy absorption in the knee was significantly higher in the planned condition as compared to unplanned condition. Motion capture data revealed that there were greater peak knee flexion and internal rotation for the planned movements. Finally, for knee and hip measures there was evidence of greater variability in the unplanned conditions.

So, we can see a few different problems here. An overemphasis on planned movements creates patterns (greater angles, rotations and energy absorption) that are likely to cause overuse injuries. Given the differences seen in the unplanned condition, the beneficial effects of variability we have been discussing, it is likely these patterns occur because the movement is overly constrained. Adding more unplanned and unpredictable movements in practice is not only more representative of what a performer is going to actually face in competition, but it also is likely to give more opportunity for them to develop this injury reducing, adaptive variability.

. . .

A similar effect can be seen when we look at the effects of perception-action *uncoupling* in practice. In a study published in 2020, Tidman and colleagues[3] compared two types of training to a non-training control group for Australian Rules Football. An *uncoupled* training group watched life-sized video projections of sequences of play and were instructed to indicate verbally which direction they would go to avoid be tackled. A *coupled* training group were presented with the same videos but executed running sidestep or crosscut maneuvers to avoid the simulated tacklers. In post-tests performed at the end of four weeks of training, the coupled group had significant reductions in peak moments of force and muscle activation (both of which have been associated with increased injury risk) that were not found in either of other two groups.

Are injuries really caused by "incorrect" technique

To what extent are injuries caused by technical flaws? Can we predict injury by doing a movement analysis and identifying these flaws in individual performers? This possibility was investigated in a study of baseball pitchers by Sutter and colleagues[4]. The authors collected MLB game videos from games played between 1920 and 2015. For each pitcher, three deliveries recorded from both a side view and behind were used. Videos were then analyzed and scored in terms of six pitching technique components including trunk angle, arm swing, posture, position at foot strike, path of arm acceleration, and finish. For each video, each of technical components was given a score from 0-4. The scores were then summed to give an overall technical scored out of 24. The final data set included 449 different players who had a total of 375 injuries.

. . .

What was found? Risk of injury significantly decreased with increase in overall delivery score (by 7.8%) and independently with increase in score of the trunk angle (by 16.5%), arm swing (by 12.0%), and position at foot strike (by 22.8%). The accuracy of the model in predicting injury was significantly better when including total delivery score compared with demographic factors like age alone. So there does seem to be some clear relationships between technique and injury. That is entirely consistent with the idea that was discussed in Chapter 9 – all skills have a relatively small set of invariant features that we can identify. Deviating from these can result in both a decrease in performance and an increased injury risk, like we saw in the ACL study at the start of this chapter. But what we must be careful about is taking this too far. As we can see in the results of this study, even when we combine all these well-known "technical flaws" in pitching there is only about 8% increase in relative risk of injury. There this clearly a lot more to the story of injury that just deviations from some ideal technique.

Adaptation to Injury not Rehabilitation

Let's turn to what happens when an athlete does get injured. I really think we should switch to using the term *adaptation* to injury instead of injury rehabilitation or recovery. Why? Rehabilitation or recovery implies that the way that we should deal with injury is by trying to get back to where we were before it happened. To me this idea is flawed and counterproductive because I think it is impossible. The bad news is you can't go home again my friends. Or as a wise person once said: "you can never step in the same river twice". Injury imposes some completely new constraints on solving a movement problem such that it really should be considered to be a completely new problem for the performer. I will get into specific examples of this in a second. But first, there is good news here. Adapting to new movement problems imposed by changing constraints is something an athlete has done and will do through their whole career -- changes produced by body growth, moving to higher skill levels, changes in rules or equipment are just a few examples. The river is always flowing -- Injury is just another part of the flow. Let's look at a couple studies that support this idea.

In an interesting paper published by Neto and colleagues in 2019[5], research investigating changes in our brain associated with an ACL injury was reviewed. It is well known that there is a high rate of ACL reinjury after surgery (of about 30%) even in young, active adults. One of the main reasons I think this occurs is the rehab or going back problem -- that is the failure to consider the new reality of the new constraints imposed on the performer. Several recent studies have shown long-term functional changes in the sensory and motor areas of the brain occur following ACL injury. These include depressed activity in the motor cortex (which regulates movement) and disrupted proprioceptive and tactile processing (which senses it). Moreover, reconstruction of the ACL does not seem to influence these neuroplastic changes, as patients with ACL reconstruction continue to show changes in neural activity. Even athletes who successfully return to their sport after ACL injury show different brain activity as compared to healthy controls.

Some research I conducted a few years ago is also consistent with these ideas. In a study published in 2015[6], I investigated the attentional focus of expert baseball position players recovering from knee injury, and pitchers recovering from elbow injury as compared to healthy controls. To achieve this, I presented a brief sound while the player was either swinging the bat or pitching a ball. On separate trials, they are asked to make judgements about the angle of their arm, the angle of their knee or the position of the ball, at the point where they heard the sound. For example, was your knee bent more than 45 degrees when you heard the beep? I then used response accuracy as a measure of attentional focus – if you have higher accuracy, I assumed it is because you were focusing on that thing.

For batting, I found that there was no difference between the injured and non-injured experts when making a judgment about their arm but there was a significant difference (with the batters recovering from ACL injury being more accurate) when making a judgment about their knee angle. This is consistent with idea that injury induces an internal focus of attention on the injured body part. For pitching, the story was a bit different. Pitchers recovering from UCL elbow surgery were more accurate at judging both their knee and elbow angle as compared to healthy controls. Thus, this injury seemed to induce a more diffuse internal focus, not just on the injured body part. I argued that this occurred because for a pitcher, how the leg moves is going to impact the stress on the elbow. Finally, I found lower variability in the timing of the movements for both the injured batters and pitchers.

So, in sum, injury seems to fundamentally alter the constraints placed on our perceptual-motor system. And these are not just simple short-term changes. We attend to different locations, have differences in the information we get, have different calibration between inputs and motor outputs, and seem to use a more constrained, visually based form of skill execution. This is the new reality, such that any "rehab" program needs to take this account and develop interventions to improve performance from this point – not try to get the athlete back to the way they moved before. Not only is going back likely to be impossible, but it is also likely to be no longer be the optimal solution for performer given their new constraints.

15

A LITTLE ABOUT MY JOURNEY & SOME EXPLORATION GUIDES FOR YOUR OWN

O ur conception of what it means to be skillful and how to best get there is changing. From an asymmetric view in which movement solutions are given to us by a coach or instructor and drilled into our brain through repetition so that they can be automatically executed. To a symmetrical view where we actively explore our environment, discover what it affords us, establish direct connections with it and self-organize. In my role as consultant, I have worked with many coaches that have decided to make the transition from traditional prescriptive coaching to using methods like the CLA and differential learning. A common piece of feedback that I have received from many is that when they make the switch the sound in the gym/court/rink/diamond/practice field immediately changes. You can literally hear the difference. There is more energy. More communication. More joy. That is why it is called *playing* sports, after all.

Of course, there are other approaches and theories. The traditional *information processing approach* to skill, which admittedly I have cast largely as a straw man throughout this book, continues to be developed by many excellent researchers and underpins the practice used by many coaches. For example, an increasingly popular theory, called *predictive processing*[1], holds that instead of trying to use internal models and knowledge to predict the outcome of our actions, our brain is attempting to predict the sensory feedback that it will receive from acting. A large amount of research is being done looking at how athletes anticipate and predict what their opponent will do next by combining and weighting different cues (e.g., the score, the opponent's body language, the ball flight) using a popular model called *Bayes Theorem*[2]. This has led to several programs for training anticipation. For many, success in sports relies heavily on the development of rich *mental models* and *understanding* of how one's actions are being controlled[3]. For example, drawing out plays on a whiteboard continues to be a popular method utilized by coaches for developing teamwork. Finally, as we saw in in Chapter 3, there is an ever-growing number of sports training technologies and programs being built of the traditional business model of skill in which it can be broken apart and de-contextualized. But to quote the immortal words of Bob Dylan: it ain't me babe.

I like to say that "I self-organized towards self-organization". I spent the first part of my career testing the predictions of traditional linear, theories of skill acquisition. I looked for the defining characteristics of THE movement solution used by expert performers. I designed experiments to show that experts had lower variability and exhibited automaticity in their movements. I even developed predictive, internal models of the control action. But then I reached a point of instability in my career. A bifurcation, like we saw in Chapter 6, that pushed me away out of the attractor valley I had been stuck in. This occurred when I started to get more serious about applying my work in the field, in particular working directly with baseball players and coaches.

I began to realize something that I strongly believe now – when you take a perception-action problem and try to solve it by appealing to some internal model or knowledge in the performer (like I was doing with my predictive models of batting) it doesn't really get you very far. It seems like you have done a lot, but you have just shifted the problem around a bit. For example, in my model I could describe how a batter takes the knowledge of the situation (the count) and combines it with the history of events and information early in the action to generate a prediction about what's going to happen. But what do they do with that prediction? Say a batter predicts the next pitch is a fastball. How does that give rise to a swing? Do they just use a pre-programmed swing that gets the bat to a certain place and time? Data I was collecting, like the study I described in Chapter 9, didn't seem to show that.

Let's return to the example of Ronaldo playing soccer in the dark I discussed back in Chapter 13. Recall the commentator's explanation: "By 500 msec Ronaldo's subconscious has interpreted Andy's body language, worked out what direction the ball will go in, calculated its speed and trajectory, and then programmed his body to reach it at the optimum moment". Does this really explain anything? How do we "pre-program our body to reach the right location at the optimum moment"? The point I am trying to make here is that explaining skill by appealing to an internal model within the performer's head just leaves you with a huge motor control problem to still solve. How is the prediction coming from Ronaldo's subconscious used to generate a movement? Who or what is receiving it?

As was the case with my own work, traditional descriptions of skill typically have very little to say about how movement is coordinated. They suffer from what I like to call the "then just move" problem. Take, for example, the popular recognition primed decision-making model proposed by Gary Klein and illustrated in Figure 15.1. Note all the elaborate steps and processing in the top part of the figure that led up to a decision. But then what happens? Oh, it is simple – we just "implement the course of action". We have reduced coordination, movement, acting (a central what it means to be skillful) to the 'A' button on a X-BOX controller. Contrast this with the constant bearing angle model shown in Figure 12.1 which provides a specific explanation about which aspect of the movement is controlled and how information is used to control it.

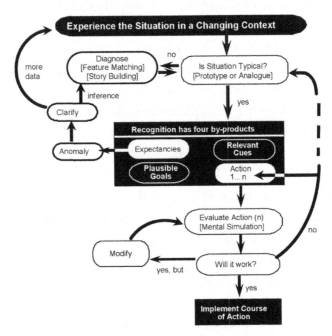

Figure 15.1 – The control of movement reduced to a single box in the Recognition Primed Decision-Making Model. From Klein, G. A. (1993).

Another critical point on my journey came when I discovered for myself something Frans Bosch[4] likes to say: "The body has very little interest in what the coach has to say". Like in the forearm flyout example I discussed in Chapter 7, through my research I had started to identify key kinematic features (what I have been calling invariants) for skills like baseball batting and pitching. But I quickly realized that I had no idea what to do with this knowledge. I discovered that there is a huge difference between *movement description*, on the one hand, and *movement instruction*, on the other. Like the results from the tennis study by Giblin et al, the athletes I was working with could not take on board my simple corrective instructions about their technique. I realized that neither I (nor the athlete's themselves) could really tell the body what to do. There was no boss. There was self-organization.

The final piece of the puzzle came when I started to look more carefully at movement variability. In one study I was doing we looked at the variability of control stick movements for pilots landing an aircraft in a flight simulator[5]. We compared novices who had never flown before at all, to highly experienced pilots with an average of more than 6000 hours of flying experience. One had more than 15000 flight hours! What we expected to find at the time was, of course, that the experts would be less variable and more stable in their movements. But we found the exact opposite! Variability was more than 1.5 times *greater* for experts than the novices. In looking at the data, we realized what was going on. The constraints we imposed on the participants (flying in very impoverished visual conditions) were encouraging the experts to search for a movement solution to land the plane. They were acting with high variability to get more information. This is something that has also been shown in sports like soccer, where exploratory movements (like scanning with the head and eyes before receiving a pass) are greater in more elite players[6].

Exploration Guides

I hope that through reading this book I have inspired you to learn more about this exciting new approach to skill. If so, I hope that that you will also adopt an approach to your own learning and development that is consistent with the ideas we have been discussing. That is, one of exploration, self-organization, and connecting with your environment. Instead of seeking out "experts" that can transmit the knowledge that you passively receive, think about experiencing it for yourself. Instead of trying to fill up your brain by reading the "key" papers or books in a field, follow your own nonlinear path guided by your own interests and your own individual constraints. Instead of looking for a new set of practice activities to just replace the drills you have been using, try things for yourself and educate your attention to the principles of effective practice design. Become a master chef, don't just follow recipes!

In that vein, the resources listed below are meant to be guides not definitive reading lists or syllabi. In my experience, *when* you read, listen to or watch something is as important as *what* resources you consume. One resource may cause a shift in your landscape making you more receptive and better able to understand the one that follows. As a personal example, it was really the third time reading some of Gibson's work that begun to understand how it fundamentally changes the way we think about everything!

Hope you enjoy the journey of exploring this fascinating topic as much as I have! Cheers for now. And (still) keep 'em coupled..

APPENDIX - EXPLORATION GUIDES

-For an alternative access to links please go to: https://perceptionaction.com/book

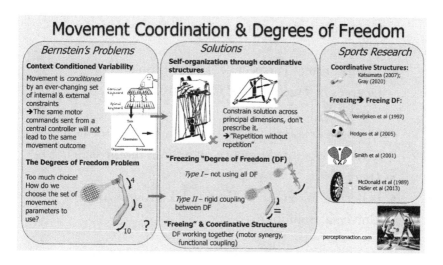

Points of Entry

- *Listen*

- The Legacy of Nikolai Bernstein I: Problems in Movement Coordination
- The Legacy of Nikolai Bernstein II: Skill Acquisition through Free(z)ing Degrees of Freedom
- *Read*
- Dexterity & Its Development
- Skill as Search
- *Watch*
- Nikolai Bernstein's Lab
- From Freezing to Freeing to Coordinative Structures: Solving the DF Problem in Skilled Movement

Paths to Explore

- *Listen*
- Freezing Degrees of Freedom as an Early Movement Solution
- Coordinative Structures in Skilled Performance
- *Read*
- The Bernstein Perspective: I. The Problems of Degrees of Freedom and Context-Conditioned Variability
- Changes in coordination, control and outcome as a result of extended practice on a novel motor skill
- *Watch*
- Is Bernstein's Freezing-Freeing DF Progression a Universal Solution?

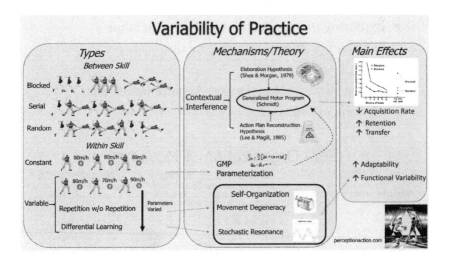

Points of Entry

- *Listen*
- The Why, What, How & When of Movement Variability
- P&A Court II: Low vs High Variability in Motor Control & Learning
- *Read*
- https://perceptionaction.com/vp/
- Does noise provide a basis for the unification of motor learning theories?
- *Watch*
- Practice Variability in Training of Motor Skills

Paths to Explore

- *Listen*
- Variability of Practice Revisited
- Interview with Damian Farrow, Victoria University/AIS, Practice Design
- *Read*

- Exploring the applicability of the contextual interference effect in sports practice
- *Watch*
- Article Review: How Do We Achieve Consistent Movement Outcomes?

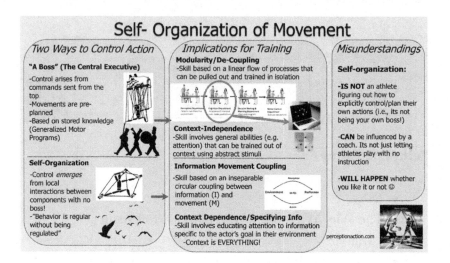

Points of Entry

- *Listen*
- Prescriptive Instruction vs Self Organization: Comparative Research & Playing Both Sides
- Reflections on the FBR Summit: Putting Self Organization into Practice
- *Read*
- Self organisation and constraints in sports performance
- What Exactly is Acquired During Skill Acquisition?
- *Watch*
- The Two Skill Acquisition Approaches: Key Differences
- Self-Organization Overview

Paths to Explore

- *Listen*
- Self Organization & Self-Regulation in Skill Acquisition: Clarifying Some Confusions
- *Read*
- The Connection Ball & Pitching: A Direct Comparison of Self-Organization vs Prescriptive Approaches
- Task Decomposition vs Task Simplification and How they Align with Skill Acquisition Approaches
- *Watch*
- Ecological Dynamics
- Ecological Skill Acquisition Terminology: Why is it so damn complicated?

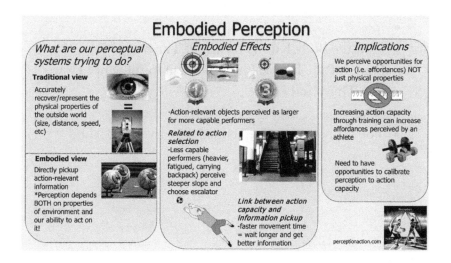

Points of Entry

- *Listen*
- Embodied Perception in Sport

- The Legacy of James J Gibson II: The Theory of Affordances & Its Application to Sports,
- Journal Club #13: Affordances
- *Read*
- Embodied perception in sport
- Information, affordances, and the control of action in sport
- *Watch*
- Affordances

Paths to Explore

- *Listen*
- How Do Action Capabilities Constrain Affordance Perception & Decision Making
- Affordance Based Control
- *Read*
- How the Body Knows Its Mind: The Surprising Power of the Physical Environment to Influence How You Think and Feel
- *Watch*
- The Embodied an Embedded Theory of the Mind

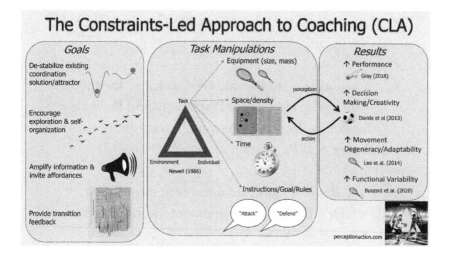

Points of Entry

- *Listen*
- The Constraints-Led Approach to Coaching I: What are Constraints?
- The Constraints-Led Approach to Coaching II: Dynamics & Representative Design
- *Read*
- The Dynamics of Skill Acquisition: An Ecological Approach
- https://perceptionaction.com/cla/
- *Watch*
- "Roots not Branches": Why the Ecological Approach is not Just a Set of Alternative Training Methods

Paths to Explore

- *Listen*
- The Constraints-Led Approach to Coaching III: Evaluating its Effectiveness

- The Constraints-Led Approach to Coaching IV: Why do we "Constrain"?
- *Read*
- When and How to Provide Feedback and Instructions to Athletes?—How Sport Psychology and Pedagogy Insights Can Improve Coaching Interventions to Enhance Self-Regulation in Training
- *Watch*
- Article Review: Contextualized Skill Acquisition Research – Dexterity development in Brazilian soccer

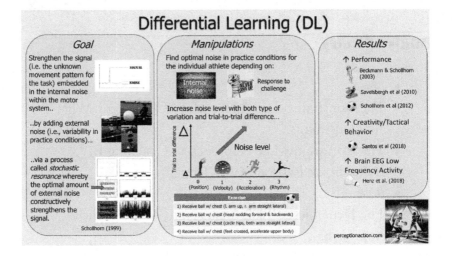

Points of Entry

- *Listen*
- Differential Learning
- Differential Learning II: Contextual Interference vs Stochastic Resonance
- Interview with Wolfgang Schollhorn, Mainz, Differential Learning
- *Read*
- https://perceptionaction.com/dl/

- Does noise provide a basis for the unification of motor learning theories?
- An Exploratory Meta-Analytic Review on the Empirical Evidence of Differential Learning as an Enhanced Motor Learning Method
- *Watch*
- Intro: Differential Learning System

Paths to Explore

- *Listen*
- Adding Variability, Execution Redundancy & "Essential Noise" to Practice with Equipment Modifications
- Differential Learning III: Clarifying Methodology, Acute Training Effects & Brain Activity
- *Read*
- The Nonlinear Nature of Learning – A Differential Learning Approach
- Comparing the constraints led approach, differential learning and prescriptive instruction for training opposite-field hitting in baseball
- *Watch*
- Does the structure and amount of variability in practice matter?

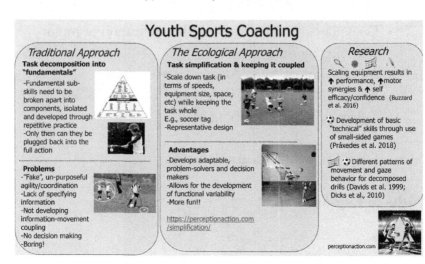

Points of Entry

- *Listen*
- Donor Sports & the Value of Non Sport Specific Practice
- Improving "impoverished practice environments"
- *Read*
- Nonlinear Pedagogy and the Athletic Skills Model
- Physical Literacy - A Journey of Individual Enrichment: An Ecological Dynamics Rationale for Enhancing Performance and Physical Activity in All
- *Watch*
- Journal Club #30: An Ecological Approach to Youth Sports Coaching & Physical Education
- Nonlinear Pedagogy

Paths to Explore

- *Listen*
- Exploring representative practice design

- Interview with Mark O'Sullivan, AIK, Affordances, Practice Design & Talent Development
- *Read*
- Nonlinear Pedagogy and the Athletic Skills Model: The Importance of Play in Supporting Physical Literacy
- Scaling junior sport competition: A body-scaling approach?
- Beyond a one-size-fits-all approach to coaching
- *Watch*
- Power of Play

Points of Entry

- *Listen*
- Constraining Vision to Educate Attention & Promote Skill Acquisition
- Are there General Perceptual-Motor Abilities? Should we be Testing & Training Them?
- Virtual Environments for Training & Understanding Sports Skills I: Why, How and When?
- *Read*
- Virtual environments and their role in developing and understanding perceptual-cognitive skills
- *Watch*
- Implementing a Constraints Led Approach (CLA) to Coaching in VR
- Article Review: Towards Individualized Optimization of Movement Coordination?

Paths to Explore

- *Listen*

- "I'm not anti-technology...I'm just pro human"
- New Research on Generalized Perceptual-Cognitive Training
- An Ecological Dynamics Assessment of Perceptual-Cognitive & VR Training in Sport
- *Read*
- Evaluating Weaknesses of "Perceptual-Cognitive Training" and "Brain Training" Methods in Sport: An Ecological Dynamics Critique
- Effectiveness and efficiency of virtual reality designs to enhance athlete development: an ecological dynamics perspective
- *Watch*
- Perception & Action Journal Club #10: VR Training for Sport

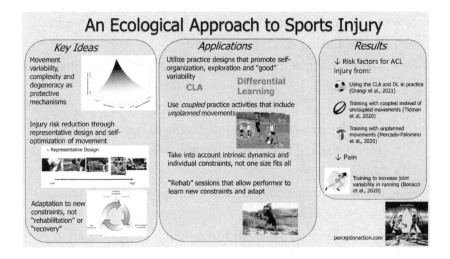

Points of Entry

- *Listen*
- An Ecological Approach to Sports Injury Prevention & Adaptation (Not Recovery),

- *Read*
- https://perceptionaction.com/injury/
- Reviewing the Variability-Overuse Injury Hypothesis: Does Movement Variability Relate to Landing Injuries?
- *Watch*
- Perception & Action Journal Club #7: Focus of Attention Instructions & Cueing in Injury Rehab
- Perception & Action Journal Club #17 – Using Biomechanics Analysis to Reduce Injury & Improve Performance

Paths to Explore

- *Listen*
- Interview with Anne Benjaminse, Groningen, Attentional Focus in Injury Prevention & Recovery
- *Read*
- Principles of Motor Learning to Support Neuroplasticity After ACL Injury: Implications for Optimizing Performance and Reducing Risk of Second ACL Injury
- Increased Risk of Musculoskeletal Injury Following Sport-Related Concussion: A Perception–Action Coupling Approach
- *Watch*
- Journal Club #16: What are "normal movements" in atypical populations?,

NOTES

Preface: How We Learn to Move

1. https://www.sportbible.com/football/news-the-incredible-training-methods-thomas-tuchel-uses-so-actual-games-f-20210506
2. https://theathletic.com/2083605/2020/09/24/fear-footballs-failure-how-the-hitting-director-behind-alec-bohm-found-a-way/#
3. Djokovic Tennis Practice Activity https://www.youtube.com/watch?v=x9eNJBzptZ0
4. Davids, K. W., Button, C., & Bennett, S. J. (2008). *Dynamics of Skill Acquisition: A Constraints-Led Approach.* Human Kinetics, Champaign, Illinois.
5. Schollhorn, W. I., Hegen, P., & Davids, K. (2012). The nonlinear nature of learning-A differential learning approach. *The Open Sports Sciences Journal, 5*(1).
6. Simons, D. J., Boot, W. R., Charness, N., Gathercole, S. E., Chabris, C. F., Hambrick, D. Z., & Stine-Morrow, E. A. (2016). Do "brain-training" programs work?. *Psychological Science in the Public Interest, 17*(3), 103-186.

1. The Myth of the One "Correct", Repeatable Technique

1. Wooden, J., & Jamison, S. (1997). *Wooden: A lifetime of observations and reflections on and off the court* (p. 201). New York: McGraw-Hill.
2. Robbins, T. (2007). *Awaken the giant within: How to take immediate control of your mental, emotional, physical and financial.* Simon and Schuster.
3. Ziglar, Z. (2007). *Better than good: Creating a life you can't wait to live.* Thomas Nelson.
4. Coyle, D. (2009). *The talent code: Unlocking the secret of skill in maths, art, music, sport, and just about everything else.* Random House.
5. "A baseball swing is a very finely tuned instrument. It is repetition, and more repetition, then a little more after that". Reggie Jackson
6. "Don't be afraid to scrape the paint off and do it again. This is the way you learn, trial and error, over and over, repetition. It pays you great dividends, great, great dividends". Bob Ross
7. Bernstein, N. A., Latash, M. L., & Turvey, M. T. (2014). *Dexterity and its development.* Psychology Press.

8. Gandon, E., Bootsma, R. J., Endler, J. A., & Grosman, L. (2013). How can ten fingers shape a pot? Evidence for equivalent function in culturally distinct motor skills. *PLOS one, 8*(11), e81614.
9. Zheng, N., Barrentine, S. W., Fleisig, G. S., & Andrews, J. R. (2008). Kinematic analysis of swing in pro and amateur golfers. *International Journal of Sports Medicine, 29*(06), 487-493.
10. Ericsson, A., & Pool, R. (2016). *Peak: Secrets from the new science of expertise.* Houghton Mifflin Harcourt.
11. Schöllhorn, W. I., & Bauer, H. U. (1998). Identifying individual movement styles in high performance sports by means of self-organizing Kohonen maps. In *ISBS-Conference Proceedings Archive*
    Figueiredo, P., Seifert, L., Vilas-Boas, J. P., & Fernandes, R. J. (2012). Individual profiles of spatio-temporal coordination in high intensity swimming. *Human movement science, 31*(5), 1200-1212.
12.
13. Horst, F., Janssen, D., Beckmann, H., & Schöllhorn, W. I. (2020). Can individual movement characteristics across different throwing disciplines be identified in high-performance decathletes?. *Frontiers in psychology, 11*.

2. We Are Built to Produce and Detect Variation

1. Shaffer, F., & Ginsberg, J. P. (2017). An overview of heart rate variability metrics and norms. *Frontiers in public health, 5*, 258.
2. Hasegawa, Y., Sumi, K., & Miura, A. (2020). State anxiety and low-frequency heart rate variability in high-level amateur golfers while putting under pressure. *International Journal of Sport and Health Science, 18*, 144-153.
3. Regan, D., & Beverley, K. I. (1980). Visual responses to changing size and to sideways motion for different directions of motion in depth: Linearization of visual responses. *JOSA, 70*(11), 1289-1296.
4. Blakemore, C., Muncey, J. P., & Ridley, R. M. (1971). Perceptual fading of a stabilized cortical image. *Nature, 233*(5316), 204-205.
5. Rucci, M., Iovin, R., Poletti, M., & Santini, F. (2007). Miniature eye movements enhance fine spatial detail. *Nature, 447*(7146), 852-855.
6. Shannon, C. E. (1948). A mathematical theory of communication. *The Bell system technical journal, 27*(3), 379-423.
7. Renart, A., & Machens, C. K. (2014). Variability in neural activity and behavior. *Current opinion in neurobiology, 25*, 211-220.
8. Waddington, G., & Adams, R. (2003). Football boot insoles and sensitivity to extent of ankle inversion movement. *British journal of sports medicine, 37*(2), 170-175.
9. Auditory Resonance demo: https://youtu.be/4pEVl2Q86QM
10. Davids, K., Shuttleworth, R., Button, C., Renshaw, I., & Glazier, P. (2004). "Essential noise"—enhancing variability of informational constraints benefits movement control: a comment on Waddington and Adams (2003). *British journal of sports medicine, 38*(5), 601-605.

11. Nadal & Carlin (2011). Rafa. Hyperion
12. Fitch, H. L. (2014). The Bernstein Perspective: I. The Problems of Degrees of Freedom and Context-Conditioned. *Human Motor Behavior: An Introduction*, 239.
13. James, C. R. (2004). Considerations of movement variability in biomechanics research. *Innovative analyses of human movement*, 29-62.
14. Bonacci, J., Fox, A., Hall, M., Fuller, J. T., & Vicenzino, B. (2020). Effect of gait retraining on segment coordination and joint variability in individuals with patellofemoral pain. *Clinical Biomechanics*, *80*, 105179.

3. The Business of Producing Movements & Why We Don't Need a Boss

1. Schmidt, R. A. (1975). A schema theory of discrete motor skill learning. *Psychological review*, *82*(4), 225.
2. "25 Years of Dynavision: A Case Study of Vision Training in Sports" https://perceptionaction.com/12d/
3. "New Research on Generalized Perceptual-Cognitive Training" https://perceptionaction.com/167-2/
4. Formenti, D., Duca, M., Trecroci, A., Ansaldi, L., Bonfanti, L., Alberti, G., & Iodice, P. (2019). Perceptual vision training in non-sport-specific context: effect on performance skills and cognition in young females. *Scientific reports*, *9*(1), 1-13.
5. https://www.ftc.gov/news-events/press-releases/2015/09/ftc-charges-marketers-vision-improvement-app-deceptive-claims
6. https://www.ftc.gov/news-events/press-releases/2016/01/lumosity-pay-2-million-settle-ftc-deceptive-advertising-charges
7. Potts, W. K. (1984). The chorus-line hypothesis of manoeuvre coordination in avian flocks. *Nature*, *309*(5966), 344-345.

4. Freedom through Constraints?!

1. Uehara, L., Button, C., Araújo, D., Renshaw, I., & Davids, K. (2018). The role of informal, unstructured practice in developing football expertise: the case of Brazilian Pelada. *Journal of Expertise*, *1*(3), 162-180.
2. Passan, J. (2016). *The arm: Inside the billion-dollar mystery of the most valuable commodity in sports*. HarperCollins.
3. Pitching in sand https://youtu.be/1RFOoyl5Tho?t=1490
4. Newell, K. (1986). Constraints on the development of coordination. *Motor development in children: Aspects of coordination and control*.
5. Milanese, C., Corte, S., Salvetti, L., Cavedon, V., & Agostini, T. (2016). Correction of a technical error in the golf swing: Error amplification versus direct instruction. *Journal of motor behavior*, *48*(4), 365-376.

6. Chase, M. A., Ewing, M. E., Lirgg, C. D., & George, T. R. (1994). The effects of equipment modification on children's self-i and basketball shooting performance. *Research Quarterly for Exercise and Sport, 65*(2), 159-168.
7. Dicks, M., Davids, K., & Button, C. (2010). Individual differences in the visual control of intercepting a penalty kick in association football. *Human movement science, 29*(3), 401-411.
8. Gray, R. (2017). Transfer of training from virtual to real baseball batting. *Frontiers in Psychology.*
9. Uehara, L., Button, C., Araújo, D., Renshaw, I., & Davids, K. (2018). The role of informal, unstructured practice in developing football expertise: the case of Brazilian Pelada. *Journal of Expertise, 1*(3), 162-180.

5. We Perceive the World in Terms of What Our Body Affords Us

1. Gray, R. (2014). Embodied perception in sport. *International Review of Sport and Exercise Psychology, 7*(1), 72-86.
2. Proffitt, D. R., Stefanucci, J., Banton, T., & Epstein, W. (2003). The role of effort in perceiving distance. *Psychological Science, 14*(2), 106-112.
3. Taylor-Covill, G. A., & Eves, F. F. (2014). When what we need influences what we see: Choice of energetic replenishment is linked with perceived steepness. *Journal of Experimental Psychology: Human Perception and Performance, 40*(3), 915.
4. Gray, R. (2014). Embodied perception in sport. *International Review of Sport and Exercise Psychology, 7*(1), 72-86.
5. Gray, R., & Cañal-Bruland, R. (2015). Attentional focus, perceived target size, and movement kinematics under performance pressure. *Psychonomic bulletin & review, 22*(6), 1692-1700.
6. Gibson, J. J. (1979). The Ecological Approach to Visual Perception. Psychology Press
7. Warren Jr, W. H., & Whang, S. (1987). Visual guidance of walking through apertures: body-scaled information for affordances. *Journal of experimental psychology: human perception and performance, 13*(3), 371.
8. Warren, W. H. (1984). Perceiving affordances: visual guidance of stair climbing. *Journal of experimental psychology: Human perception and performance, 10*(5), 683.
9. Franchak, J. M., & Adolph, K. E. (2014). Gut estimates: Pregnant women adapt to changing possibilities for squeezing through doorways. *Attention, Perception, & Psychophysics, 76*(2), 460-472.
10. van Knobelsdorff, M. H., van Bergen, N. G., van der Kamp, J., Seifert, L., & Orth, D. (2020). Action capability constrains visuo-motor complexity during planning and performance in on-sight climbing. *Scandinavian Journal of Medicine & Science in Sports, 30*(12), 2485-2497.

11. Gray, R. (2013). Being selective at the plate: Processing dependence between perceptual variables relates to hitting goals and performance. *Journal of Experimental Psychology: Human Perception and Performance, 39*(4), 1124.
12. Eves, F. F., Thorpe, S. K., Lewis, A., & Taylor-Covill, G. A. (2014). Does perceived steepness deter stair climbing when an alternative is available?. *Psychonomic bulletin & review, 21*(3), 637-644.

6. Learning as Search, the Laws of Attraction and the Tim Tebow Problem

1. Schöner, G., Zanone, P. G., & Kelso, J. A. S. (1992). Learning as change of coordination dynamics: Theory and experiment. *Journal of motor behavior, 24*(1), 29-48.
2. Zanone, P. G., & Kelso, J. A. (1992). Evolution of behavioral attractors with learning: nonequilibrium phase transitions. *Journal of Experimental Psychology: Human perception and performance, 18*(2), 403.
3. Clark, J. E. (1995). On becoming skillful: Patterns and constraints. *Research quarterly for exercise and sport, 66*(3), 173-183.
4. Tim Tebow's throwing mechanics https://youtu.be/w9R7vd78q1A
5. Gladwell, M. (2008). *Outliers: The story of success*. Little, Brown.

7. New Ways of Coaching I: The Constraints-Led Approach (CLA)

1. Aguinaldo, A. L., & Chambers, H. (2009). Correlation of throwing mechanics with elbow valgus load in adult baseball pitchers. *The American journal of sports medicine, 37*(10), 2043-2048.
2. Giblin, G., Farrow, D., Reid, M., Ball, K., & Abernethy, B. (2015). Exploring the kinaesthetic sensitivity of skilled performers for implementing movement instructions. *Human Movement Science, 41*, 76-91.
3. Gray, R., Allsop, J., & Williams, S. (2013). Changes in putting kinematics associated with choking and excelling under pressure. *International Journal of Sport Psychology, 44*(4), 387-407.
4. Pelz, D. (2000). *Dave Pelz's putting bible: the complete guide to mastering the green* (Vol. 2). Doubleday Books.
5. Masters, R. S. (1992). Knowledge, knerves and know-how: The role of explicit versus implicit knowledge in the breakdown of a complex motor skill under pressure. *British journal of psychology, 83*(3), 343-358.
6. Lola, A. C., & Tzetzis, G. (2020). Analogy versus explicit and implicit learning of a volleyball skill for novices: The effect on motor performance and self-efficacy. *Journal of Physical Education and Sport, 20*(5), 2478-2486.
7. Connection ball https://youtu.be/mSK7PnKm6Hg

8. Newell, K. M. (2003). Change in motor learning: a coordination and control perspective. *Motriz, Rio Claro, 9*(1), 1-6.
9. Lee, M. C. Y., Chow, J. Y., Komar, J., Tan, C. W. K., & Button, C. (2014). Nonlinear pedagogy: an effective approach to cater for individual differences in learning a sports skill. *PloS one, 9*(8), e104744.

8. New Ways of Coaching II: Differential Learning

1. Schollhorn, W. I., Beckmann, H., Michelbrink, M., Sechelmann, M., Trockel, M., & Davids, K. (2006). Does noise provide a basis for the unification of motor learning theories?. *International journal of sport psychology, 37*(2/3), 186.
2. Schollhorn, W. I., Hegen, P., & Davids, K. (2012). The nonlinear nature of learning-A differential learning approach. *The Open Sports Sciences Journal, 5*(1).

9. Good Vs Bad Variability, Optimal Movement Solutions & Effective Self-Organization

1. Guimarães AN, Ugrinowitsch H, Dascal JB, Porto AB, Okazaki VHA. Freezing Degrees of Freedom During Motor Learning: A Systematic Review. Motor Control. 2020 Mar 28;24(3):457-471. doi: 10.1123/mc.2019-0060. PMID: 32221040.
2. Hodges, N. J., Hayes, S., Horn, R. R., & Williams, A. M. (2005). Changes in coordination, control and outcome as a result of extended practice on a novel motor skill. *Ergonomics, 48*(11-14), 1672-1685.
3. Kato, T., & Fukuda, T. (2002). Visual search strategies of baseball batters: eye movements during the preparatory phase of batting. *Perceptual and motor skills, 94*(2), 380-386.
4. Klostermann, A., Vater, C., Kredel, R., & Hossner, E. J. (2015). Perceptual training in beach volleyball defence: different effects of gaze-path cueing on gaze and decision-making. *Frontiers in psychology, 6*, 1834.
5. Vine, S. J., Moore, L., & Wilson, M. R. (2011). Quiet eye training facilitates competitive putting performance in elite golfers. *Frontiers in psychology, 2*, 8.
6. Can Assisted Movement Facilitate Skill Acquisition? https://perceptionaction.com/96-2/
7. Gray, R. (2020). Changes in movement coordination associated with skill acquisition in baseball batting: Freezing/freeing degrees of freedom & functional variability. *Frontiers in Psychology*
8. Yang, J. F., & Scholz, J. P. (2005). Learning a throwing task is associated with differential changes in the use of motor abundance. *Experimental brain research, 163*(2), 137-158.
9. Morrison, A., McGrath, D., & Wallace, E. S. (2016). Motor abundance and control structure in the golf swing. *Human movement science, 46*, 129-147.

10. A New Perspective on What It Means to Be Creative

1. https://www.macleans.ca/news/canada/record-setting-high-jumper-who-invented-technique/
2. Orth, D., McDonic, L., Ashbrook, C., & van der Kamp, J. (2019). Efficient search under constraints and not working memory resources supports creative action emergence in a convergent motor task. *Human movement science, 67*, 102505.
3. Working Memory Capacity Test https://www.cognifit.com/cognitive-assessment/battery-of-tests/wom-asm-test/sequential-test
4. Renshaw, I., Glazier, P., Davids, K., & Button, C. (2005). Uncovering the secrets of The Don: Bradman reassessed. *Sport Health, 22*(4), 16-21.
5. Caso, S., & van der Kamp, J. (2020). Variability and creativity in small-sided conditioned games among elite soccer players. *Psychology of Sport and Exercise, 48*, 101645.
6. Torrents Martín, C., Ric, Á., & Hristovski, R. (2015). Creativity and emergence of specific dance movements using instructional constraints. *Psychology of Aesthetics, Creativity, and the Arts, 9*(1), 65.

11. Youth Coaching: The Problem with Cones & Making Practice Fun Again

1. Soccer tag https://youtu.be/w3RaGq66ebM
2. Dicks, M., Button, C., & Davids, K. (2010). Examination of gaze behaviors under in situ and video simulation task constraints reveals differences in information pickup for perception and action. *Attention, Perception, & Psychophysics, 72*(3), 706-720.
3. Gray, R., Regan, D., Castaneda, B., & Sieffert, R. (2006). Role of feedback in the accuracy of perceived direction of motion-in-depth and control of interceptive action. *Vision research, 46*(10), 1676-1694.
4. Goodale, M. A., & Milner, A. D. (1992). Separate visual pathways for perception and action. *Trends in neurosciences, 15*(1), 20-25.
5. Bruno, N., & Franz, V. H. (2009). When is grasping affected by the Müller-Lyer illusion?: A quantitative review. *Neuropsychologia, 47*(6), 1421-1433.
6. Stevenson, K. P., Smeeton, N. J., Filby, W. C., & Maxwell, N. S. (2015). Assessing representative task design in cricket batting: Comparing an in-situ and laboratory-based task. *International Journal of Sport Psychology, 46*(6), 758-779.
7. Albert Pujhols vs Jennie Finch https://www.youtube.com/watch?v=gm9iZnqGMvY

8. Buzzard, T., Garofolini, A., Reid, M., Farrow, D., Oppici, L., & Whiteside, D. (2020). Scaling sports equipment for children promotes functional movement variability. *Scientific reports*, *10*(1), 1-8.

9. Arias, J. L. (2012). Influence of ball weight on shot accuracy and efficacy among 9-11-year-old male basketball players. *Kinesiology*, *44*(1).

10. Pellett, T. L., Henschel-Pellett, H. A., & Harrison, J. M. (1994). Influence of ball weight on junior high school girls' volleyball performance. *Perceptual and motor skills*, *78*(3_suppl), 1379-1384.

11. Buzzard, T., Garofolini, A., Reid, M., Farrow, D., Oppici, L., & Whiteside, D. (2020). Scaling sports equipment for children promotes functional movement variability. *Scientific reports*, *10*(1), 1-8.

12. Práxedes, A., Del Villar, F., Pizarro, D., & Moreno, A. (2018). The impact of nonlinear pedagogy on decision-making and execution in youth soccer players according to game actions. *Journal of human kinetics*, *62*, 185.

13. https://perceptionaction.com/196/

14. Strafford, B. W., Van Der Steen, P., Davids, K., & Stone, J. A. (2018). Parkour as a donor sport for athletic development in youth team sports: insights through an ecological dynamics lens. *Sports medicine-open*, *4*(1), 1-6.

15. Han, J., Waddington, G., Anson, J., & Adams, R. (2015). Level of competitive success achieved by elite athletes and multi-joint proprioceptive ability. *Journal of Science and Medicine in Sport*, *18*(1), 77-81.

16. Alexander, K. R. (2013). Some Seed Fell on Stony Ground: Three Models-Three Strikes!.

12. What Are We "Acquiring" Anyways? The Nature of Expertise, Automaticity and Direct Learning

1. Wooden, J., & Jamison, S. (1997). *Wooden: A lifetime of observations and reflections on and off the court* (p. 201). New York: McGraw-Hill.

2. Peale, N. V. The Power of Positive Thinking. Simon & Schuster

3. Sharman, B. (1965). *Sharman on basketball shooting*. Prentice-Hall.

4. Ronaldo playing in the dark https://youtu.be/_AIaX2Lg_os

5. Chardenon, A., Montagne, G., Buekers, M. J., & Laurent, M. (2002). The visual control of ball interception during human locomotion. *Neuroscience letters*, *334*(1), 13-16.

6. Ingold, T. (2002). *The perception of the environment: essays on livelihood, dwelling and skill*. routledge.

7. Jacobs, D. M., & Michaels, C. F. (2007). Direct learning. *Ecological psychology*, *19*(4), 321-349.

8. Mohebbi, R. & Gray, R. (2007). Perceptual-motor control strategies for left-turn execution. *Driver Assessment 2007 Proceedings*. Iowa City, IA.: University of Iowa Public Policy Center.

9. Lee, D. N., Lishman, J. R., & Thomson, J. A. (1982). Regulation of gait in long jumping. *Journal of Experimental Psychology: Human perception and performance, 8*(3), 448.
10. Warren Jr, W. H., Young, D. S., & Lee, D. N. (1986). Visual control of step length during running over irregular terrain. *Journal of Experimental Psychology: Human Perception and Performance, 12*(3), 259.
11. Fajen, B. R., & Warren, W. H. (2003). Behavioral dynamics of steering, obstacle avoidance, and route selection. *Journal of Experimental Psychology: Human Perception and Performance, 29*(2), 343.
12. Fitts, P. M., & Posner, M. I. (1967). Human performance.
13. Araújo, D., & Davids, K. (2011). What exactly is acquired during skill acquisition?. *Journal of Consciousness Studies, 18*(3-4), 7-23.

13. The Evolving Role of Technology and Data in Supporting Skill Development

1. Chin Up Goggles https://www.youtube.com/watch?v=28MSHkqpaKw
2. Dunton, A., O'Neill, C., & Coughlan, E. K. (2019). The impact of a training intervention with spatial occlusion goggles on controlling and passing a football. *Science and Medicine in Football, 3*(4), 281-286.
3. Oudejans, R. R. (2012). Effects of visual control training on the shooting performance of elite female basketball players. *International Journal of Sports Science & Coaching, 7*(3), 469-480.
4. Oudejans, R. R., Heubers, S., Ruitenbeek, J. R. J., & Janssen, T. W. (2012). Training visual control in wheelchair basketball shooting. *Research Quarterly for Exercise and Sport, 83*(3), 464-469.
5. Stroboscopic glasses https://www.youtube.com/watch?v=4txQ_ZWfsZI
6. Wilkins, L., & Appelbaum, L. G. (2020). An early review of stroboscopic visual training: Insights, challenges and accomplishments to guide future studies. *International Review of Sport and Exercise Psychology, 13*(1), 65-80.
7. Gray, R. (2019). Virtual environments and their role in developing perceptual-cognitive skills in sports. In *Anticipation and decision making in sport* (pp. 342-358). Routledge.
8. Gray, R. (2018). Comparing cueing and constraints interventions for increasing launch angle in baseball batting. *Sport, Exercise, and Performance Psychology, 7*(3), 318.
9. Gray, R. (2020). Comparing the constraints led approach, differential learning and prescriptive instruction for training opposite-field hitting in baseball. *Psychology of Sport and Exercise, 51*, 101797.
10. Fleisig, G. S., Diffendaffer, A. Z., Ivey, B., & Aune, K. T. (2018). Do baseball pitchers improve mechanics after biomechanical evaluations?. *Sports biomechanics, 17*(3), 314-321.

11. Felton, P. J., Yeadon, M. R., & King, M. A. (2020). Optimising the front foot contact phase of the cricket fast bowling action. *Journal of Sports Sciences*, *38*(18), 2054-2062.

12. Boyd, J., & Godbout, A. (2010). Corrective sonic feedback for speed skating: A case study. Georgia Institute of Technology.

13. Gray, R. (2015, September). The Moneyball problem: what is the best way to present situational statistics to an athlete?. In *Proceedings of the Human Factors and Ergonomics Society Annual Meeting* (Vol. 59, No. 1, pp. 1377-1381). Sage CA: Los Angeles, CA: SAGE Publications.

14. Gray, R., Orn, A., & Woodman, T. (2017). Ironic and reinvestment effects in baseball pitching: How information about an opponent can influence performance under pressure. *Journal of Sport and Exercise Psychology*, *39*(1), 3-12.

15. Wulf, G. (2013). Attentional focus and motor learning: a review of 15 years. *International Review of sport and Exercise psychology*, *6*(1), 77-104.

16. Zachry, T., Wulf, G., Mercer, J., & Bezodis, N. (2005). Increased movement accuracy and reduced EMG activity as the result of adopting an external focus of attention. *Brain research bulletin*, *67*(4), 304-309.

17. Yeoman, B., Birch, P. D., & Runswick, O. R. (2020). The effects of smart phone video analysis on focus of attention and performance in practice and competition. *Psychology of Sport and Exercise*, *47*, 101644.

14. Injury Prevention & Adaptation (Not Rehabilitation!)

1. Orangi, B. M., Yaali, R., Bahram, A., Aghdasi, M. T., van der Kamp, J., Vanrenterghem, J., & Jones, P. A. (2021). Motor learning methods that induce high practice variability reduce kinematic and kinetic risk factors of non-contact ACL injury. *Human Movement Science*, *78*, 102805.

2. Mercado-Palomino, E., Richards, J., Molina-Molina, A., Benítez, J. M., & Espa, A. U. (2020). Can kinematic and kinetic differences between planned and unplanned volleyball block jump-landings be associated with injury risk factors?. *Gait & posture*, *79*, 71-79.

3. Tidman, S. J., Lay, B., Byrne, S., Bourke, P., & Alderson, J. (2020). Reducing anterior cruciate ligament injury risk factors by training perception: How vital is maintaining the perception-action coupling?. *ISBS Proceedings Archive*, *38*(1), 440.

4. Sutter, E. G., Orenduff, J., Fox, W. J., Myers, J., & Garrigues, G. E. (2018). Predicting injury in professional baseball pitchers from delivery mechanics: a statistical model using quantitative video analysis. *Orthopedics*, *41*(1), 43-53.

5. Neto, T., Sayer, T., Theisen, D., & Mierau, A. (2019). Functional brain plasticity associated with ACL injury: a scoping review of current evidence. *Neural plasticity*, *2019*.

6. Gray, R. (2015). Differences in attentional focus associated with recovery from sports injury: does injury induce an internal focus?. *Journal of sport and exercise psychology*, *37*(6), 607-616.

15. A Little about My Journey & Some Exploration Guides for Your Own

1. Clark, A. (2013). Whatever next? Predictive brains, situated agents, and the future of cognitive science. *Behavioral and brain sciences*, *36*(3), 181-204.
2. Gredin, N. V., Bishop, D. T., Williams, A. M., & Broadbent, D. P. (2020). The use of contextual priors and kinematic information during anticipation in sport: toward a Bayesian integration framework. *International Review of Sport and Exercise Psychology*, 1-25.
3. Filho, E., Tenenbaum, G., & Yang, Y. (2015). Cohesion, team mental models, and collective efficacy: towards an integrated framework of team dynamics in sport. *Journal of sports sciences*, *33*(6), 641-653.
4. Bosch, F. The Anatomy of Agility. HHMR Media.
5. Gibb, R., Schvaneveldt, R., & Gray, R. (2008). Visual misperception in aviation: Glide path performance in a black hole environment. *Human factors*, *50*(4), 699-711.
6. Aksum, K. M., Pokolm, M., Bjørndal, C. T., Rein, R., Memmert, D., & Jordet, G. (2021). Scanning activity in elite youth football players. *Journal of Sports Sciences*, 1-10.

ACKNOWLEDGMENTS

I would like to thank my two main career mentors: Barrie Frost from Queens University and David Martin Regan from York University.

-RG

ABOUT THE AUTHOR

Rob Gray is a professor at Arizona State University who has been conducting research on and teaching courses related to perceptual-motor skill for over 25 years.

He received his MS and PhD from York University in Canada with a focus on the visual control of movement. He has served as an expert consultant with Nissan Motor Corp, the US Air Force and with several sports teams and organizations.

In 2007 he was awarded the Distinguished Scientific Award for Early Career Contribution to Psychology from the American Psychological Association.

He is also the host and producer of the popular Perception & Action Podcast. Explore the episodes at https://perceptionaction.com/

f facebook.com/perceptionactionpodcast

𝕏 twitter.com/ShakeyWaits

🅟 patreon.com/perceptionaction

ⓐ amazon.com/author/robgrayasu